How To Write
for the
How-To Market

How To Write
for the
How-To Market

Suzanne Ruthven

**COMPASS
BOOKS**

Winchester, UK
Washington, USA

First published by Compass Books, 2013
Compass Books is an imprint of John Hunt Publishing Ltd., Laurel House, Station Approach,
Alresford, Hants, SO24 9JH, UK
office1@jhpbooks.net
www.johnhuntpublishing.com
www.compass-books.net

For distributor details and how to order please visit the 'Ordering' section on our website.

Text copyright: Suzanne Ruthven 2013

ISBN: 978 1 78099 722 3

A CIP catalogue record for this book is available from the British Library.

Design: Stuart Davies

Printed and bound by CPI Group (UK) Ltd, Croydon, CR0 4YY

We operate a distinctive and ethical publishing philosophy in all
areas of our business, from our global network of authors to
production and worldwide distribution.

CONTENTS

About the Author

How To Write for the How-To Market is based on Suzanne Ruthven's inimitable tutoring style, and as she says: *"I'm a commissioning editor for a publishing house and a magazine editor, but first and foremost, I'm a writer, and so my allegiance is always going to be with serious writers who want to see their work in print."*

Editor of the popular quarterly creative writing magazine, *The New Writer* (which she produces in partnership with publisher, Merric Davidson), and author of over 30 books on spiritual, country and self-help matters, including three writers' guides, *Signposts for Country Living*, *The Good Divorce Guide*, *The Dating Game* and *Exploring Spirituality*, she has also contributed articles to a variety of publications as diverse as *The Lady*, *The Countryman*, *Prediction* and the *Funeral Director's Journal*. In 2011 she became commissioning editor for Compass Books, a writers' resource imprint of John Hunt Publishing, who have published her latest title, *Life-Writes: Where Do Writers Get Their Ideas From?*

Chapter One

Plotting & Planning

Everyone, at sometime in their lives, needs to learn how to do something they have never attempted before. From planning a wedding, preparing an after dinner speech, considering a career change, writing a stage play, taking up a new hobby, organising a holiday, improving a life-style, joining a horseracing syndicate, making a WWII Woolton pie, down-sizing a home ... the list is endless. And if anyone has ever asked how we managed to achieve any of these things, then we have something to write about.

Wherever we live in the world, How-To writing can run from magazine fillers on how to organise a successful car boot (yard) sale to a full-length self-help book on, for example, *Exploring Spirituality*. Or as one online contributor commented in an interview in the *Daily Telegraph*:

"A lot of us have expertise without realising it. Put a question about something you know well into an online search engine and you'll be surprised how many people have asked the same question before. If other people don't know how to do something and you do – then you could write about your expertise."

It goes without saying, of course, that to write convincingly on a subject and be able to impart the appropriate information means that we are following the old adage of 'writing about what we know' for the benefit of our readership.

Write About What We Know
As we mature, and gain more experience, then our How-To

guides will develop further in-depth insights into our various fields of expertise. For example: when I wrote my first writing guide I was editing a magazine, and with one published full-length book to my name, the aim being to produce a practical nuts and bolts guide to starting a writing career, with plenty of additional advice from other tutors, editors, authors and freelance writers. The second guide was written to support the increasing number of writers' workshops I was tutoring; as the first book had passed its sell-by date and out of print, another completely different book was required. *Life-Writes*, was my third creative writing book, and written to coincide with my acting as commissioning editor for Compass Books, so that as an author I always have something new on offer and not stuck in the time-warp of constantly regurgitating previously published material, or resting on my laurels.

My specialist genres are the countryside and the mind, body and spirit market, so the next title was *Exploring Spirituality*, which catered for the growing interest in alternative religions and the decline in both traditional religious and spiritual values. Having discovered the successful formula for writing and presenting How-To books, the next on the list was *The Good Divorce Guide*, followed by *WLTM: The Dating Game*, which grew out of the long conversations with a close friend who runs an introduction agency for country people. *Signposts For Country Living* is a guide to avoiding the pitfalls often experienced by 'incomers' trying to establish themselves in rural communities. These will be followed by *How To Write for the Pagan & MB&S Markets* and *How to Write for Countryside Publications*.

Other writers from around the globe with various different levels of expertise, will be able to tackle How-To subjects pertaining to their own life-styles – for example: yachting/canal/river boating; restoring a vintage 57 Chevrolet; learning to surf; backpacking in the Outback; where to study abroad; overcoming personal or social problems, culture shock –

and each country will have its own publishing houses that cater for How-To, Self-Help and Self-Improvement titles. This does not mean that we can only write for publishers or publications within our own borders – *our* market is the entire English-speaking world.

Qualified by Life

As we can see from my own personal selection, How-To books can cover *every* aspect of Life - family, hobbies, career, life-style – and, needless to say, our expertise is drawn from our own experiences, or the experiences of those close to us. The particular hook (or spin) that we put on the narrative to cater for a specific target market, however, will depend on where we see ourselves fitting into the picture. It's not enough to write on a subject with mere enthusiasm because all How-To, Self-Help and Self-Improvement topics need to reflect 'life as it is lived' by those who have already lived it. And imparted to the reader in a way that will encourage them to follow our guidelines or example.

In fact, when reading a proposal or preparing a reader's report, I study the author's *biography* before turning to the text – regardless of how intriguing the title or synopsis. I want to know right from the start, the writer's antecedents and whether they are eligible to write on the appropriate level for the subject in question. Many writers attempt to pass themselves off as being more knowledgeable or experienced than they really are – and this can be a minefield for a publisher's reader who may not be completely *au fait* with the subject under discussion. This doesn't mean to say that a beginner isn't capable of imparting sound How-To advice, but it must be written from the *beginner's perspective*, so that the reader identifies with the trials and tribulations of someone just starting out.

In the How-To and Self-Help market, the author's background is just as important as the content of the book

or article. You have to sell yourself, not just the idea.

Obviously, unless we are highly qualified by experience or education, we must give even more thought as to the direction our instruction will take. In the case of *The Good Divorce Guide* and not having any legal training, it needed to reflect the divorce process from a personal self-help position, and with as many different viewpoints as possible, including the slant of also giving it male reader-appeal. *WLTM: The Dating Game* was co-authored, and offered a practical guide to agency dating for both men *and* women in the forty-plus age range, as my friend felt these were the people who wouldn't be so comfortable with online or speed-dating. *Signposts For Country Living* was written from my 'born and bred' country perspective. Again, by taking a magazine approach of an informal, inclusive style rather than a patronising catalogue of do's and don't's.

We also need to give some thought to the writing *style* we intend to adopt, which will be largely governed by the subject matter. Black humour would be inappropriate in 'How To Arrange Your Own Funeral' but the odd sprinkling of under-takers' cautionary tales could help to lighten what otherwise could be a doleful read in a feature-length article or book on the subject. Nevertheless, even the most serious of subjects can have an injection of light heartedness to lessen the load, but avoid jokey, 'hail-fellow-well-met' humour that could be judged as being in poor taste where emotive subjects are concerned. Neither would levity be acceptable in academic or technical writing – which can still come under the How-To heading if you are qualified to write about them.

Show Not Tell

The informal, inclusive style of using 'we' and 'our' also lends itself perfectly to Self-Help and Self-Improvement books, because we are implying that we've been there and are now using the t-shirt for dusters. We are identifying with the reader in their present situation, and they with us. We're settling down for a cosy chat rather than a lecture because the patronising, exclusive style that uses 'you' all the time, often comes across as smug, school-marmy and unsympathetic. In true writing tutorial tradition, **we are showing, not telling.**

How-To and Self-Help titles are possibly one of the easiest of books to write and sell, because we are writing from personal experience, and will already have the necessary contacts to embellish the text with the additional experiences of a wide variety of other people to provide depth, corroboration, humour and anecdote. Neither do we need to write the chapters in strict sequence because each one has a slightly different slant or approach. We may have sufficient research material to hand to finish one chapter, while another takes much longer because of the need to follow up, and obtain more material or permissions. By rule of thumb, we'll know if we have enough material for a full-length book on our chosen subject if we can comfortably write 45,000 words, broken down into approximately 10 separate chapters; divided by approximately 10 sub-headings for each chapter. This means each chapter will contain around 4,500 words.

There are, however, a number of other rules to observe and it pays to understand these *before* settling down to write. It's also important to invest in a quality newspaper at least once a week, because quite a lot of a non-fiction writers' stimulus comes from a study of what's in the news. It gives us ideas for all aspects of imparting information and more often than not, a clearer picture of our target readership. Read the regular columns that reflect current viewpoints on the multitude of social activities and lifestyles and you'll be surprised how much information/ideas they can generate.

And a final point to remember is that it is easy for able-bodied people to write How-To's that cater for disabled readers. People with disabilities are still interested in exactly the same things and as Stephanie Green pointed out in 'Writing For Disability Markets' for *Freelance Market News*: "There are a wide variety of disability publications, from glossy lifestyle magazines ... informative how-to guides ... Remember you are writing for people with disabilities, not just about them, and they love being entertained just like everyone else." Study a few back issues of the magazines before submitting, and be aware of the different nuances in the writing requirements.

Synopsis and Full Chapter Breakdown

Once we've started to develop the idea for a full-length How-To book, *that's* when we start to trawl the marketplace for a suitable outlet. Because How-To publishers usually have their own formula dictating how the text should be presented, and it's not a good idea to present them with the complete typescript, since this may require a complete re-write to comply with their individual house-style.

This is where we do our homework and investigate every publisher in the genre who is likely to be interested in our subject. Spend some time with the writers' handbooks and examine *all* the entries in the 'How-To' category, i.e. How-To literary agents and publishers, including the small presses. This exercise is five-fold because it:

- identifies the publishers who may be interested in our subject matter, and whether they have anything similar already in print, or planning stages;
- gives an insight into the competition, together with examples of the various different approaches to similar subjects already in print;
- provides us with a working check list and ready-made chapter breakdown, subject by subject;

- prevents us from wasting time writing the full text that may have to be completely re-written;
- identifies publishers and agents in other parts of the English-speaking world who may be interested in our work.

For example: as we would expect, there were numerous books on divorce but most were written from the legal perspective, so my book covered coping with the shock effects and aftermath of the separation-divorce process. There were several biographical books covering the dating industry, so our book was specifically aimed at the forty-plus age group that make up the bulk of clients in the more traditional agencies. There have also been dozens of books about moving to the country but seldom written *by* country people for the benefit of 'in-comers'. And there are hundreds of writers' guides written by experienced novelists, playwrights, poets and journalists ... so there has to be a fresh twist on an original idea.

All this valuable information *must* be included in the synopsis because a publisher needs to see immediately whether the proposed book has a place on their titles list, and where it sits in the market place. Our 'hook' must be different to anything other books in the same genre are offering. In other words, *show* that we've done our homework prior to making contact and prove that we are professionals, not someone working our way through the writers' handbooks, hoping to strike it lucky with some barely thought-through proposal.

By now we should have the book mapped out so that we have a rough idea of where we are going with it. There should also be a bulging file of cuttings, information sheets and statistics to support our research, and enough time spent on the project for us to be able to prepare a full chapter breakdown, which is self-explanatory from the publisher's point of view. The following is an example of a full chapter breakdown for a 'work in progress' careers book; it shows exactly how the book will evolve, and what information will be included in the text – and where.

I Want to Work in Horse Racing

Chapter One: The Sport of Kings
I want to work in Horse Racing
Racing in UK and Ireland
On the Flat
Steeplechasing
The Jockey Club
British Horseracing Authority
Wetherbys
Channel 4 Racing
Be realistic in following the dream
Would I be suitable?
Chapter Two: The Trainers
The Power and the Glory
Small is beautiful
Getting on with the job
A Day in the Life of
Newmarket
Middleham
Lambourne
Polo
Arab Racing
Point to Pointing
Chapter Three: Runners and Riders
What the experts say
The Jockey School
Riding out
Work riding
The Apprentice
The Stable Jockey

The desk jockey
Chapter Ten: Finding Alternatives
Where did it go wrong?
The knee-jerk reaction
Redefining your goal
Job satisfaction
Serving the apprenticeship
Putting experience to good use
Pause for thought
Tinseltown
Where do I go from here?
Summary

As the publisher can see immediately, every aspect of a career within the horse racing industry has been included from the stable-yard to racecourse catering, ground staff, and media opportunities. All it needs is an accompanying letter giving the background and qualifications of the author ... and I've sold every single one of my How-To books on the strength of a similar proposal.

The next step is to study the **backlist** of all How-To, Self-Help/Improvement publishers in the country where you live and who may be interested in considering your proposal. Trawl through the writers' handbooks for publishers, small presses, and literary agents from the UK, the USA, Australia and Europe who specialise in How-To and Self-Help books and, where possible, obtain a copy of the writers' submission guidelines for each one, together with a complete list of their current titles.

Check out the latest How-To and Self-Help/Improvement titles in your local bookstores and library, and see how each one prefers the typescript presented to comply with their individual house-styles. The first thing that will be apparent is the layout of each book. Yesterday's How-To books had plenty of bullet-points, coloured boxes and side-bars for emphasis, with case histories and anecdotes separate from the main body of the text – although for today's books this layout complicates the setting up of an e-book version. All of them *will* require that the author has practical experience in the field in which they write, but often this is the first step on the publishing ladder for a large number of new writers.

Contacts & References

All types of How-To and Self-Help writing will also require the information contained within the text to be supported by contact details, websites and referrals so that the reader is provided with instant follow-up access to the information given. In full-length books this information can be included as an appendix, while articles usually provide the details in the main text, at the foot of the article, or in separate side bars.

Websites give in-depth information and contact details that eliminate the need to expand on each individual service. Give as many different sites/addresses as possible so that you are listing a good cross-section of services, opinions, providers, etc.

If we are prominently featuring one particular service remember that *we* are giving a personal recommendation for this company or organisation, and therefore have a responsibility to the reader to make sure our information is reliable and accurate. Unlike a lot of celebrity adverts, don't endorse anything of which you have no personal experience.

Note: All examples of the How-To articles included in *How To Write For The How-To Market* are previously published, although the contact information has been deleted in these examples to save space. All were published with the relevant contact details given as a footnote or side bar where appropriate.

The Spin-Offs

Once our How-To book has been published there are various spin-offs that will help promote sales and earn higher royalties. Magazine and newspaper editors will be keener to accept article proposals from an author whose book has just been, or is about to be released, because the publisher's acceptance is an endorsement of our writing ability. This can be a feature in the form of an extract from the book, or a shorter article adapted from a single chapter. Needless to say, an editor is hardly likely to make any payment for the piece since it is an extract and not 'previously unpublished'. Nevertheless, it is well worth the lack of fee in order to get our name (and book title) out there amongst the reading public, especially in specialist magazines where there will be a higher proportion of interest in our subject.

Short, sharp snippets of How-To information can provide valuable fillers and most magazines and newspapers are eager for such material. Handy hints and tips can be drawn from all kinds of gardening and kitchen craft, while simple health and beauty fillers can be aimed at women's magazines and the women's pages in newspapers. Any magazine or newspaper, in fact, can be the target for How-To fillers and 'Letters to the Editor' - and this is the type of beginner's material we will be producing for the exercises in this book.

There are also online websites in the UK and the USA that specialise in How-To material, such as eHow.com or wikihow.com – trawl the internet under 'How-To sites' including www.websearch.about.com; or www.makeuseof.com. Make sure the company really will pay for any material they use – some make tempting promises but move the goalposts if contributors appear to be reaching the targets too easily. Choose your site carefully and that the potential earnings are ongoing, since the more pages we write, the more money we can earn from advertising revenue. Let's log on and have a look at how easy it is ...

The How-To Article

The following are examples of articles published on How-To websites and continue the horseracing theme from material taken from the synopsis and chapter breakdown given earlier. There are also other completely different horsey How-To's published elsewhere, aimed at people at completely opposite ends of the equine spectrum that were spin-offs from the original career guide proposal.

The background in horseracing comes from my partner, who is a former Newmarket work-rider and headman, with a life time's experience working with and riding racehorses. We have both mixed with the equestrian fraternity all our lives so lots of material to draw on, together with other angles and ideas – such as 'How To Organise A Car Boot Picnic' (see Chapter Seventeen). The ideas could possibly appeal to publishers wherever there is a popular horseracing industry – the idea will travel; only the technicalities and/or organisations will differ from country to country.

How To Join a Horse Racing Syndicate

Owning and maintaining a racehorse is a very expensive business and although joining a racing syndicate doesn't come cheap, it does provide a way of living your dream. Undoubtedly this a very exciting hobby but the cost of buying your own horse and then funding the stable bills, veterinary costs and racing fees can become very expensive. However, being involved in a syndicate is not just about sharing costs ... it is also about the excitement of the racecourse and sharing the joy of winning.

- Nothing beats the thrill of watching your own thoroughbred in your syndicate's colours pass the winning line first – and should you be interested in starting out in horseracing ownership, the best way is to begin is with a syndicate.
- A syndicate, often arranged by a racing yard, is a group of

individuals owning shares in a horse being trained for racing, which enables all syndicate members to share the benefits and the costs.

- The people in the syndicate pool together funds to buy a share in the racehorse and have it trained to race, with each person paying a substantial monthly fee.

- Syndication, however, allows you to get involved in the excitement of horseracing without it hugely impacting on your life, because the trainer is responsible for the day-to-day care and management of your horse.

- One of the most famous of the syndicates is The Champagne Club, formed over 22 years ago and which has grown to become one of the most successful. Newmarket based Alan Bailey is the Club's trainer and with his excellent tips the members have more than covered their investment with some terrific gambles landed during the year. Alan is also quite a character and has hosted some great social events for the Club members at his Newmarket based stables.

- The Club also arranges social events at the racecourses and as a shareholder you will be kept fully informed of your horse's racing plan by text, plus you will receive an ownership certificate with photograph. Racecourse badges (subject to availability) will be provided at a reduced cost when your horse races and hospitality will be arranged whenever possible. Check out their website and see what's on offer and how a good syndicate should be run.

Conclusion

Horseracing provides an opportunity to meet with friends, new associates and fellow enthusiasts in a fun, entertaining and social atmosphere. You may even get up on the winner's podium! Ask for syndicate details at your local racing yard but be wary of a syndicate that will not allow you to visit the stables and see your horse.

Or a much simpler idea:

How To Care for Riding Tack

Regular care and polishing of riding tack not only means that the bridle and saddle are well turned out – it also means that regular attention is paid to the wear and tear on the leather to prevent accidents and skin abrasions on the horse.

You will need:

Saddle soap with glycerine
A clean sponge
Warm water

- Saddle: A cheap and badly made saddle is a false economy, as it will certainly give the horse a sore back – a saddle should be made to fit both the horse and rider. It should be wiped over after each ride with a damp sponge to clean off mud and sweat, and worked with saddle soap to keep the leather supple. Check all straps and buckles for wear and loose stitching.
- Girth: A poor girth can cause 'girth galls' which are troublesome and the horse cannot be ridden until the cure is complete. This can be avoided if care is taken in tightening the girths, and keeping them clean at all times. Have several in use so that the horse is never ridden with a damp girth. Check daily for wear and tear.
- Bridle: Since this carries the bit and reins, it is essential that the bridle is checked daily for safety, because it restrains the horse and directs its movements. Check the leathers and buckles after every ride, wiping over with a damp sponge and working with saddle soap to keep the leather supple.
- Bit: Wipe over with hot water to remove saliva and prevent sore mouths.

- Numnah: A felt, rubber or sheepskin pad cut in the shape of, though rather larger than the saddle and worn under it to prevent undue pressure from the saddle on the horse's back. Always have a spare so that the horse is never ridden with a damp numnah; wash weekly to remove sweat and mud.

Conclusion

Well-maintained tack safeguards your horse's health and your own personal safety.

Never use second-hand tack with dried-out leather and rusty buckles; check all stitching, leather straps and buckles on a regular basis. Remember poorly maintained tack can kill!

It doesn't matter if you're not ready to go for a full-length book at this stage because the exercises will help you focus on the other opportunities in the How-To market. And by the end of this book you should have built up an impressive folio of How-To pieces and be fully conversant with the different approaches required by editors and publishers. How-To articles and books are all about imparting solid, reliable, practical information in the simplest possible way – with the maximum amount of guidance. It doesn't matter what the subject, someone, somewhere will be asking "How do I ...?"

Let's Get Started ...

These exercises are designed to give the opportunity to build up your portfolio and earn some extra income at the same time. Needless to say, you will have to demonstrate that you have the ability to write quality and useful How-To guides, and all articles chosen for publication would have to adhere to each individual site or publication's submission guidelines – for example:

- All articles must explain and describe to the reader how to do or achieve something.

- Each article must comply with the layout and template of the publisher, magazine, newspaper or website, usually comprising of an introduction explaining what will be achieved by following the instructions, broken down step-by-step. Each step must comprise of actionable instructions, followed by a sound conclusion.
- The articles must be written in a way that makes it clear and easy to understand, using correct grammar, spelling (US or UK English, for example) and punctuation.
- If other sources have been used to research the article, such as other publications or websites, this information should be included in the article where appropriate.
- All information must be correct, and make sense to the reader.
- The articles should be all your own work and not copies of, in whole or in part, other articles posted or published elsewhere, without being accredited.

Don't worry about getting it right the first time, but do check any target-market websites to make sure that your article isn't a duplicate of something already published, as magazines often carry details of previous issues. These short, snappy How-To's *can* be interchangeable between magazines or newspapers and online websites, so plenty of opportunity to make a double killing on the fees. But do conform to the house-style of each individual target.

NB: All book titles used as examples in the text are taken from the various different imprints of John Hunt Publishing. Go to www.johnhuntpublishing.com and read the 'blurb' for each book as a further guide to books already in publication. The categories given in bold throughout the text (i.e. see Arts) suggest that some topics could also suit other market outlets.

Chapter Two

Arts & Entertainment

The field of arts and entertainment is boundless, and so this is a good place to instil one very important rule for the writer to school him or herself into automatically observing. **Never write about the first thing that comes into your head** – because everyone else will have come up with the obvious, too! This is an exercise in 'word association' and many of the How-To examples given in this book will, on the surface, appear to be completely unrelated to the chapter heading. This is deliberate and another lesson of what we call 'thinking outside the box', and previously explored in *Life-Writes: Where Do Writers Get Their Ideas From?*

Art

'The Arts' cover the whole spectrum of creative art forms such as creative writing, crafts, painting, sculpture, theatre, music, dance, etc – although different aspects of theatre, music and dance, if viewed from another perspective, could also come under another heading (see **Entertainment** or **Career)**. There are, of course, the practical nuts and bolts ideas of how to write fiction, or find an agent, but the 'Art' heading could just as easily include 'How To Organise A Community Arts Project' or simply 'How To Take Care of Artists' Brushes' – it's the simple ideas that catch the editor's eye, not the grand ones.

This means, of course, that we don't have to be a qualified teacher or instructor to impart knowledge. Enthusiastic amateurs are often better at recognising the need for basic How-To advice because they are still at the stage where there are silly, niggling little things that require explanation, and which many people would be too embarrassed to ask about for fear of ridicule in more exalted company. What artistic interests do you have?

Can they be turned into How-To material? For example, the following doesn't tell us the obvious of 'how to write a novel' – but shows how to sell it ...

How To Write a Novel Synopsis

It's often said by writers that it's harder to write a synopsis than it is to write a complete book. This is because the synopsis must encapsulate an entire story in order for a publisher or agent to judge whether they wish to see the full typescript.

Nevertheless, a well-written synopsis, together with the first three chapters of your novel will tell them all they need to know about your writing in the first instance.

- Generally speaking, a synopsis should be no longer than an A4 page – single spacing = approx 500 words.
- Only introduce the principal characters and restrict yourself to a thumbnail sketch of each in one sentence per person. Even if the narrative is character driven, a publisher or agent is going to be more interested in the plot.
- Ask yourself: what is my story about? Now retell the story as if you were answering the question asked over dinner - anymore than 500 words and your listeners' eyes would begin to glaze over with boredom.
- Don't write the synopsis in a chapter by chapter style – tell the story as a piece of well crafted mini-fiction.
- And yes ... publishers/agents DO want to know how the story ends! Don't make the mistake of thinking that if they want to know how it ends they will send for the complete typescript. It doesn't work like that.
- Make sure you include important moments of intense highs and lows, but avoid drawn out descriptions of who's doing what to whom.
- Make an opening statement about when and where the

story is set. This immediately identifies the period/setting in the reader's mind.

- For a non-fiction book the rules are still the same because you are still telling a story but without characters. Give the reason for writing a new book about the subject, and why you think it will have reader appeal. Also give a hint of any new or original information you have obtained that adds a spark to the subject and justifies a publisher adding the book to his lists.

- A synopsis for Self-Help and How-To books can be submitted as a chapter by chapter breakdown, because the publisher can immediately see from the chapters how the book will progress. Opening sample chapters will give an example of your writing.

- Put the finished synopsis away in a drawer for a few days before sending it off. Sometimes we can produce something better if we allow our ideas to simmer.

Conclusion

The importance of a good synopsis cannot be stressed strongly enough. Avoid leaving the writing of it until the last minute or you'll look upon it as a job to be got out of the way without too much thought. A rejection or acceptance may hinge on how much effort you've put into writing it. Keep it short and snappy by studying the blurb on the cover of recently published books and see how the publishers have encapsulated the story, in order to grab the browser's interest in just a few words. Warning: A long, rambling synopsis can mean instant rejection of your book.

Creative writing offers one of the widest opportunities for full-length 'art' tutorials and the Compass Books' stable mates of *How To Write For The How-To Market* include Lynne Hackles' *Handy Hints For Writers*; Jay Ramsay's *The Poet In You*; Linda M James's *How To Write & Sell Great Short Stories*; Simon Whaley's *The*

Positively Productive Writer; Susan Palmquist's *How To Write Romance*; Nik Morton's *Write A Western in 30 Days*; Sarah-Beth Watkins' *Telling Life's Tales* or Deborah Durbin's *So You Want To Be A Freelance Writer*. The list is growing all the time and we can immediately see how many different permutations there are in one single aspect of Art, even using art – particularly creative writing as therapy (see **Health**). Can you produce the same for any of the other disciplines?

Is there any element of the 'Arts' that could provide you with enough material for How-To articles or a full-length How-To book? How to learn to paint. Or how to run theatre or dance workshops; poetry or reading group. Or pursing a career in music or dance? How to market rural crafts (see Business or Work)?

Marketplace

The focus for How-To articles in this genre will more than likely be a niche-market that caters for like-minded souls – so plenty of market research is needed to locate the right outlets. Look for magazines, blogs and websites that cater for actual participants in the various art forms, particularly creative writing, dance, music, theatre, art and art history magazines – as well as online How-To sites, and monthly regional and local events' publications. Not to mention the professional health care and disability publications that use art as therapy. This won't be a very lucrative marketplace but it would look good in your portfolio. If you have enough material for a full-length book, however, have a look at the How-To publishers' submission guidelines and send a proposal, especially if it's for something outside the box – such as Marsha Scarbrough's *Medicine Dance: One woman's healing journey into the world of Native American Shamanism* or Robert William Barry's *The Music of the Future*. And don't forget here's an opportunity for how to encourage children to take up reading, music and dance (see **Education**) that might suit parenting and educational publications.

Entertainment

The dictionary definition for entertainment is: *the act of entertaining; the reception of and provision (of food and drink) for guests; that which entertains or amuses; a performance or show intended to give pleasure.* So, by rule of thumb, we can see that the subject heading for 'entertainment' can be defined as being the organisation of an event that caters for those who wish to be entertained.

Depending on the ambition of the organiser and the number of people involved, we are looking at anything from how to arrange a simple supper party or summer barbeque, to concerts, amateur dramatics, art exhibition, readers' groups, pantomime, garden fete, gymkhana, children's summer camp, community picnic, or street party. Anything, in fact, that involves getting a few people together with a view to enjoying themselves. The organisation of many forms of entertainment arises simply out of like-minded people getting together and arranging their own amusement. The following idea was based on some of the activities of a social group that I once belonged to whilst living in London:

How To Organise a Theatre/Concert Party Group

There may come a time in our lives when we find ourselves alone – a divorce, bereavement, moving house, change of job – but find that the opportunities for meeting new, like-minded friends presents a bit of a problem. If you're interested in music and/or theatre the solution might be easier than you think. You can form your own theatre/concert party group by advertising in the local free newspapers, company or community notice boards and local radio.

- A theatre/concert group usually meets once a month to attend a show, play or concert, dividing the cost of transport between the number of people in the party. The initial members will therefore be restricted to the largest vehicle your local taxi firm can provide.

- Choose the wording of your advertising carefully, as you don't want to be mistaken for a singles' group - but make it clear that only serious theatre-goers need apply. Keep an open mind about gender, martial status, age, etc., or you could find yourself overlooking interesting people at the expense of conformity.

- Arrange a casual meeting in a public place initially so that the new group can casually discuss ideas and make suggestions. Prepare a 'membership form' that interested members can complete by stating their likes and dislikes.

- Familiarise yourself with the current season's events at local theatres and have a rough idea of the productions you would initially propose booking. Check with the box office regarding availability and as soon as you have two or three people signed up – book the tickets.

- Don't be tempted to arrange parties more than once a month as some of the group may not be as well-heeled as others, and it could cause resentment or embarrassment if they have to be left out.

- It doesn't always have to be a West End production – many community theatres have quite an impressive programme at a fraction of the ticket cost. The Questors (West Ealing, London) for example, is the largest community theatre in Europe, with an audience membership of around 3,000, of whom around 600 are actively involved in productions. It offers members a wide range of activities and social events, in addition to a season of around twenty shows a year, a variety of courses and workshops, and a regular programme of visiting companies. There is also a lively social club in The Grapevine Bar.

- Lunchtime concerts are also worth considering, as many of the musicians are those heard regularly on Radio 3 – but with modestly priced tickets. Also to be considered are the open-air concert-picnic evenings during the summer months.

- As the group gets to know each other better, activities could be extended to include pre-theatre drinks (to ensure everyone is in one place for the transport pick-up) or if nothing appeals at the theatre, organise a supper party instead.

- It may turn out that two or three of you prefer to 'keep it small' and, if that is the case, don't risk spoiling things by adding people who may not fit in.

Conclusion

Remember that this idea is about forming new friendships for social evenings, so don't be afraid to refuse 'membership' to anyone who doesn't gel with the existing group. For just a little bit of initial effort, you may find that you widen your opportunities for a social life quite considerably in a very short time.

This concept could also be expanded to include group visits to historic venues and gardens, or race meetings – or even 'how to start an active singles group'. Anything that requires organisation for the benefit of a community interest – be it large or small, from village fetes or private supper parties – it provides the writer with something to write about. And the greater the subject, the better the chances for turning it into a full-length book, such as David Stubb's *Fear of Music: Why People Get Rothko But Don't Get Stockhausen*. Although Sinead Murphy turned things on their head with *The Art Kettle*, and asked whether community arranged arts projects were another form of mind control – and tells us how to spot it!

There is also the Self-Help aspect of explaining why joining something like a local theatre group as a volunteer can provide the right social outlet needed by those who suddenly find themselves alone, through a change in personal circumstances or having decamped to a strange town because of a career move. You don't have to be the extrovert actor-type – even the shyest of people can be part of the team selling programmes, working 'front of house', sewing buttons on costumes in wardrobe, or painting scenery. Being a stranger in London many years ago, I also joined the Questors' Theatre 'front of house' team and that provided a vital lifeline in making new friends on my doorstep (see **Friends**) and offered a 'safe' bar that I could visit any evening on my own when I fancied some company.

Have you had any experience at organising local community events? What problems did you encounter? And how did you solve them? How would you go about explaining the work involved to other interested parties? How did joining a local group help you?

Marketplace

Whenever a group of people get together to organise something for the benefit of others ... *That's Entertainment!* And there's plenty to write about because local, regional and national newspapers, women's magazines and online sites are always on the lookout for fresh ideas to enhance the community spirit. This is an ideal opportunity for the 'born organiser' to earn some money from his or her talents from simple How-To articles, to a full-length book. There are quite a few 'arts and entertainment' magazines that are worth exploring for market outlets – not to mention the Internet and *Willings Press Guide* for additional information.

Build Your Portfolio

For the purpose of clarity we are using the bullet point approach, which shows the step-by-step stages required by the majority of How-To pieces, and immediately reveals the simplicity or depth appropriate for each individual subject. Not all publications will use the bullet point system but when compiling your article use it to sort out the different points in order of instruction or importance - and then write up the piece to suit your target market, including any online opportunities. **Remember to keep copies of everything you have published in a special folder.**

Exercise 1: Arts

Let's keep it simple for the first exercise and try to come up with a How-To hint for a creative writing magazine. What difficulties did *you* experience when starting out as a beginner writer – and more to the point, how did you solve them? Was it a simple idea that gained you extra time for writing? Have you a simple system for cataloguing ideas? Submit your first How-To exercise to the writing magazine of your choice as a filler, or something for the Letters page.

Exercise 2: Entertainment

Your second exercise needs to be a bit more ambitious and could appeal to the same target market but possibly from a different angle. 'How To Chose the Right Writers' Course' was snapped up by Howopia but so might a piece coming from the opposite viewpoint – 'how to encourage the perfect workshop participant' – that told folk how to get the most out of a writers' conference or workshop. Advising people what to expect and how to behave at an event or function would also come under the heading of entertainment: such as 'how to dress for ... the Henley Regatta; a Kenwood open air concert; Ascot'. Or Glyndebourne, where the dress code differs between the summer festival and the winter tour (see **Style**) ... and make sure you check your facts. Or just a simple piece of 'home entertainment' advice, such as how to downsize your book, CD or DVD collections (see **Home**).

Chapter Three

Business & Corporate

Writing for the business, professional, industrial or commercial world obviously requires a considerable amount of inside expert knowledge and/or experience to be a credible journalist. If we have financial, legal, scientific or engineering skills, then there are dozens of opportunities within the trade and professional journals but for the rest of us, there are writing opportunities - in the role of the customer/consumer.

Like most people of my age, I've worked in a variety of different companies over the years: advertising and public relations; sub-editor on a house journal; in London's rag-trade; and international conference organising – all of which have their own tales to tell - but what was an insignificant, but recurring business problem that was common to all aspects of business? Communication!

Business

The most common occurrence is enclosing a covering letter with documentation but for some even this can be extremely daunting – while on the other hand others will prepare some rambling discourse containing all manner of irrelevances that can result in the recipient scratching their head in utter bewilderment. This is one of those occasions where 'keep it simple' is the order of the day and was taken up by an online How-To site:

How To Write A Cover Letter

A cover letter means exactly what it says – it is a letter that usually accompanies another document(s), and provides the basic details relating to the sender.

- Cover letters need to be short, concise and to the point, rather than some rambling discourse that gives everything from your blood group to your grandmother's maiden name.
- Where possible, try to find out the name of the person to whom your letter should be sent. In publishing, for example, the opening 'Dear Sir or Madam' can be the kiss of death for any submission. Without reading any further it indicates that the writer hasn't bothered to check whether their work suits that particular magazine or publisher's list – or the name of the appropriate editor.
- If sending a letter to a large company 'Dear Sir or Madam' letters may also end up in the rubbish bin, simply because no one knows who to give them to. The person who opens the post hasn't got time to read through a letter and accompanying material before making a studied decision as to who gets it – and even if they do, it may not be the right person.
- Your cover letter should include your name, address, telephone number and email address as a header, i.e. all contact details.
- The main body of the text should state what is being sent for consideration/perusal and your reason for submitting it. Any biographical details should be kept to a minimum and only pertinent to the submission itself.
- A cover letter should never be longer than an A4 sheet of paper.

Conclusion

Too much information may just convince a prospective employer or organisation that they couldn't work with you, no matter how impressed they might be with your work or experience.

It's such a simple idea that it was almost an embarrassment to propose it as a How-To article but the fact remains that a lot of people don't know how to write a cover letter and are often too embarrassed to ask. Simple How-To business tips like this can be aimed at consumer magazines and newsletters, and the Letters page of the weekly women's magazines. Alternatively, a large company may employ you in a capacity that constantly reveals particular communication problems from the outside world, and put you in a position to offer advice without revealing your identity, or compromising any company business ethics.

Have you any handy hints that you could share with fellow consumers when dealing with business problems? Or do you have a complaint you feel needs airing? Can you offer advice on establishing more efficient communication with businesses and/or organisations?

Marketplace

The first thing that springs to mind are the hundreds of 'Letters pages' – for example: Why is there only one cashier on duty in main post offices and banks on market days, when everyone collects their pension/benefit/family allowance, etc? Or why do hospitals make a 1.00 pm appointment for *everyone* attending on that day? Not only would this strike a chord in your local newspaper, it might even be acceptable in the house journal of the local health authority, bank or post office. It might not be strictly 'business' but we are still the customer, client or consumer on the receiving end and these organisations are supposed to be run with business efficiency. Often employment or staffing issues would also come under this category, which could find an outlet in small business or appropriate trade publications. A full-length How-To run any type of business could be of interest to a publisher – similar to Brian Barfield's *Modern Day Selling* or Philip Bradbury's *Planting and Growing Your Own Business: The Idiot-Proof Guide to Profit and Business Growth*.

Corporate

Specialists in the corporate world write for the financial sections of the broadsheets and finance publications – but the ordinary man or woman in the street often needs advice on how to approach these multi-billion pound giants. Rarely can anyone go through life without resorting to letters of complaint, usually about financial or utility companies but unless we know how to cope with their stonewalling, or blank refusals to co-operate, this can be a tedious and costly business. We may feel that we can't fight the big boys and that the whole thing is a waste of time but there often *is* someone to fight in our corner ... so what about 'how to complain to the Ombudsman' or any other 'watchdog' set up to monitor industry on the public's behalf?

To my convoluted way of thinking, it's also at corporate root-level that one of the fastest-growing crimes is expanding and that's identity theft. This is where thieves target personal financial details via old bank statements and utility bills that we may unwittingly discard. This is an extremely serious subject and so the article needs to be an in-depth look at how we can protect ourselves.

How To Avoid Identity Theft

Perhaps we are too trusting because identity theft is still on the increase and has been recently identified as the UK's fastest-growing crime. According to the Cabinet Office, this 'white collar' criminal activity costs the UK at least £1.3bn every year and alarmingly is the most difficult to prevent. A typical example is where the victim's identity is taken over in order to access personal credit accounts, or open new ones in that name. Although banks and financial institutions are continuously introducing more and more highly sophisticated methods to deter identity thieves, those successfully targeted can often take up to 14 months to realise they are victims. It has been estimated that it takes on average some 300 hours to put the records straight and costs in the region of £500 to clear a victim's name, so what can we do to prevent identity theft in the first place?

- Identity theft occurs when someone 'obtains a loan from a financial institution by impersonating someone else'. The finance companies often have no fail-safe method of discovering that the thief is pretending to be someone else, especially if the original documentation cannot be verified (as is frequently the case with online, mail, telephone, or fax-based transactions).
- In reality, this particular crime is considered 'non-self-revealing', and the authorities would only be able to trace the thief if they were foolish enough to have the money mailed direct to themselves. In most instances the thief keeps the money, the finance or credit card company is never repaid, the victim is wrongly accused of defaulting on a loan that they never authorised ... and given a poor credit rating as a result!
- It may also come as a surprise to learn that over seventy-five per cent of our UK waste contains personal or business information that can be used by fraudsters, who need to obtain personalised documents about an individual in order to impersonate them. On the domestic front they can do this by: stealing mail or picking up rejected junk mail; copying or taking personal documents from your home or workplace; rummaging through rubbish bins containing personal information; advertising bogus jobs (either full-time or work from home based) to which the victims will reply with their full name, address, telephone numbers, and banking details, etc; changing your address thereby diverting billing statements to another location to either obtain legitimate information, or to delay discovery of fraudulent accounts.
- The easiest solution is to invest in a shredder and make a

habit of destroying anything personal that can be traced back to you and your family. Even junk mail from finance companies can be useful to an identity thief and how many of us just throw the envelopes in the bin unopened? Shredders come in all sizes and prices, from the monster than will crunch credit cards and computer discs to the low cost, single sheet machines that can be bought at the Post Office. The shredded paper can then be re-cycled in a variety of ways from parcel packing and composting to pet bedding, but it will no longer be of any use to a potential thief.

- Never leave utility bills, bank and credit card statements where visitors can see them, and never leave credit cards or cheque books in unattended handbags or briefcases.

- Don't dispose of junk mail (offering finance, loans or credit cards, etc) with your printed name and address in the rubbish. Burn or shred every piece of unwanted paper that contains personal details.

- Be wary of giving credit or debit card and bank details online. A PayPal account is the safest method for online payments.

- Always shield the keypad of ATM machines from anyone standing behind you, or from any device that has been planted by identity thieves above the keypad. Replace cards inside your wallet before moving away from a counter or cash machine.

- Don't carry a written note of PIN numbers in the same wallet as your bank, credit or debit cards.

- Get into the habit of regularly checking your credit card and bank statements for unfamiliar transactions. If you discover anything suspicious, report the matter immediately.

Conclusion

Identity thieves don't discriminate between the young or old, wealthy or those on a pension; they don't even care about the financial standing of their victim ... all they need is a name and a few personal details to use for fraudulent purposes, make sure that no one can gain access to your mail. The fact that there's no money in your account isn't a safeguard – it's the banking details the thieves want, not direct access to your cash. Prevention is better than suffering the horrors of identity theft, and getting into the habit of destroying unwanted personal documentation might just prevent your life from being torn to shreds. You might think it can't happen to you ... but it can.

Here we are making it clear that banks and financial institutions *are* constantly upgrading their systems and cannot be held responsible for our own security failings. Nearly every permutation of 'personal detail' has been taken into account and because of the seriousness of the subject matter, we cannot afford to scrimp on the information – and to offer a superficial article that didn't address all the preventative measures people can take to avoid identity theft, would quickly reveal our amateur writer status!

Advice on How To obtain compensation or reimbursement from the larger institutions is often useful, such as in the circumstances of the big banking computer-crash that affected thousands of customers in the UK and Ireland.

Have you had any experiences in trying to reclaim monies or compensation from holiday companies for example? Or attempted to return faulty goods for refund? Have you found it necessary to contact the Ombudsman or any other government agency for assistance? If so, your story could encourage others to complain if you explain how to go about it.

Marketplace

This type of article appears regularly in the financial pages of newspapers and, providing it is written in layman's terms, many of the women's and retirement magazines could be interested. There's a vast difference between submitting handy hints and a serious How-To piece – so give it plenty of thought and use quotes from financial agencies to add authority to your writing. On the full-length feature and book front (and as a former conference organiser), an idea that springs to mind is: 'how to arrange corporate hospitality' – arranging the entertainment by business companies of potential clients by wining and dining them at prestigious sporting events. In the current financial climate, businesses are cutting back but there may be dozens of ways of getting better value for money. Under the corporate category we could also look at the various career opportunities open to graduates – see **Careers** and **Education** – which may appeal to the educational supplements and magazines.

Build Your Portfolio

You don't necessarily have to be involved in corporate business to be affected by its day-to-day workings, and even the smallest business concern can be affected by financial cut backs. Money-saving and waste disposal tips would always be of interest – one company recently found it was more economical to re-introduce a 'tea-lady' than have staff wandering off to the canteen for extended tea-breaks. Listen to your family and friends when they talk about goings-on in the workplace and see if you can turn this into a How-To idea. My involvement with the Financial Ombudsman was on behalf of an elderly friend who had an on-going dispute with one of the major banks – the whole sorry mess landed in a draw but he finished up with an apology and a generous cheque in compensation.

Exercise 3: Business

This heading can also cover personal 'business' that involves advising on how to apply for things – i.e. government grants, enterprise allowance schemes, tax credits, etc – or changes to government legislation in these areas. Or hints and tips on how to dress, conduct yourself, etc when attending for different types of interview. Small business magazines, online How-To sites, and local newspapers could offer an outlet for this type of writing.

Exercise 4: Corporate

A much more restricted market but by thinking outside the box we can usually come up with some customer/consumer viewpoint that could be interesting to an editor. Make a study of the financial pages in the weekend broadsheets and see if they stimulate any ideas that you can adapt for the newspapers' Letters pages, an online How-To site, or even the corporation's own house journal.

Chapter Four

Computers & Electronics

Most of us wouldn't presume to write on the subject of computers or electronics but there must be thousands of people who, like myself, manage the day-to-day basics of using a computer and finding our way around the Internet. And, although there always comes a time when we think we'd like a website of our own, the cost of finding someone to set it up and manage it on our behalf, usually puts us off.

Whether we like it or not, the modern world is almost totally electronic and more and more aspects of life are now only accessible by computer – have you tried to renew a passport lately via the British Embassy? Electronic publishing is also the order of the day with all submissions, communications, contracts and proofs being up and down-loaded with impunity. The great Kindle debate rages on and we even have to fill-in type-boxes with weird and wonderful letter and number sequences to prove we're not robots - and confirm we *are* humans generating the email!; while mobile-phones, i-Pods and Pads are mini-computers in themselves.

Computers

The following How-To article appeared in a creative writing magazine, aimed at those writers in a similar position, and who needed an idiot's guide to building your own website in the simplest way possible. As far as other ideas are concerned – what problems have *you* encountered on the web and had to sort out for yourself? Computer-eze is a must for twenty-first century living but you don't have to have a degree in computer sciences to have something to say on the subject. When you find an easy solution – share it!

How To Set Up a Website

Everyone, it seems, needs a website these days but the lack of technical know-how and the cost of employing a professional web-builder may appear to be prohibitive – especially for those not of the computer generations. There are, however, numerous companies who can provide easy access to setting up a website. LetsHost, for example, is just one of those who provides a complete package - for a very reasonable cost and a first-rate support team. Just follow these simple steps:

- The first thing you'll need is a 'domain name' by which your site will be known on the internet. By clicking on to the 'Domain Names' tab you can search for available names and selected whether you require a .com or .co.uk address depending on whether your business is global or national. Once you've made your selection and received confirmation that the address you require is available, pay by credit/debit card or via PayPal and the domain name is registered to you for a year.
- The next step is to set up a 'Hosting Plan' for the website and email addresses. LetsHost offers a complete hosting plan that is designed to suit the needs of almost every user, from beginner to experienced web user. This can be paid for monthly by invoice if required.
- Choose a template design from the hundreds on offer and select the package that is right for you. You can begin with the 3-page Starter Website and upgrade at a later date as you become more familiar with the system. There is a 'test-drive' facility that enables you to mock-up a complete website without commitment and to see how easy it is to use.
- The LetsHost infrastructure and support teams are based in Ireland, they are approachable and friendly – and can usually deal with any problems promptly. Phone 00353

(0)1653 5032 and ask your questions if you have any doubts.

- By paying a modest yearly fee for the Web-builder site, you can then select the template you wish to use and begin to give it your own identity by changing the background colour, adding your own picture and text. This is all done by following the easy step-by-step instructions ... until you decide to 'Publish'. With new sites this may take between 24-48 hours before your site is accessible on the Web.

- By using your site's personal user name and password, you can edit or add further text at any time – and the additions are almost instantaneous.

- Packages range from a 1-page business card site; a 3-page starter website; a 10-page personal website; a 30-page small business package (with a demo available) to a 70-page Ecommerce website. All the different packages and fees are clearly shown on the website.

Conclusion

With computer technology becoming more and more confusing, the LetsHost web-builder packages are surprisingly simple to set up, edit and up-grade. In addition, and what is even more important, the support team are second to none, usually able to correct any mistakes you've made, even as you speak. And the price is right!

In this example I am recommending one particular company, which most magazines would probably view as 'advertorial' and not be willing to pay a fee for. I now have two websites and three e-mail addresses managed by this company, so have no hesitation in recommending them, since they've always been at the end of the phone to guide me through what to *me* were insurmountable problems – and to them minor hiccups.

LetsHost also helped with the horrendous legal minefield of selling a 'domain name' to an American company. The whole procedure was so nerve-racking and jargon-laden that I would have given up halfway through the negotiations if it hadn't been for them. The article was a way of saying 'thank you'. Having said that, I would *not* attempt to write 'how to sell a domain name', simply because I cannot remember a single thing about the whole painful operation – and even though I completed every stage of the proceedings myself, I couldn't write anything about it that made sense.

What is it about computers that drives you mad as you fumble and stumble around the internet? You won't be alone and your How-To hints could help solve someone else's problem. What about 'How To use the internet café?'

Marketplace

The obvious target market for writers would be the writers' magazines but editors often suffer from over-kill on beginners' viewpoints about computers, so try looking further afield – although there are always opportunities in the computer magazines for the technically more experienced. For the uninitiated, Sarah-Beth Watkins has produced *The Writer and the Internet*, a full-length How-To book for writers who wish to find their way around the internet with one eye on the market-place; while for those with publication in mind, Susan Palmquist came up with *The E-Book Writer's Guide & Directory*.

Beginners' laments probably wouldn't interest editors of the numerous computer magazines but the occasional piece of humour just might help to break up the tedium of technical pieces. 'How to buy a new computer' that puts together the advice given by different sales-people could make for interesting reading – especially where the advice is conflicting – a sort of *'Fried Green Tomatoes at the Internet Café'*. There is another market place in looking at **Careers** in IT and **Education** – particularly Further Education courses for older people who want to learn about computers and the Internet.

Electronics

On the surface this would seem like another minefield for the amateur, but we 'know-nots' have a greater advantage over the 'know-alls', because we usually have a vast storehouse of difficulties that 'techies' would never dream of viewing as a problem.

Even the most pathetic of techno-idiots realises, for example, that all the monthly bills for the new digital television, telephones and broadband can reach staggering proportions if we don't do our homework. So we cruise the web and find out how to save money on the most basic of domestic electronic stuff ... and we write about it for publication.

How To Make Savings on Digital TV, Telephone & Broadband

Rising utility bills are constantly putting extra strain on our finances but there are ways of making huge savings on TV, broadband and phone deals as providers fight for business.

1   Recent research by Ofcom-accredited comparison service Simplifydigital.com showed that 84% of TV, broadband and phone customers could save more than £445 per year.
2   A free and impartial service like Simplifydigital.com can be a big help in identifying the best deal in your area, with free expert advice available 7 days a week, and more than 6,000 deals to chose from.
3   Alternatively, the *Telegraph* Digital Service can compare over 11,000 deals currently on offer.
4   Moneysupermarket.com lists the best broadband deals they can find from all major providers. You can find them quickly and easily on the site, and start saving money

immediately if you get your broadband, digital TV and home phone together in one package.

5   Guardian digital Comparison also offers to find the best deals by comparing a wide range of services.

Conclusion

Despite the potential savings, people often put off moving to a better deal because of the hassle of switching over to a new service. This is why Simplifydigital.com's free switching support service is proving to be so popular, because their UK-based consultants are on hand every step of the way, up to the new service up and running in your home. Check with other providers to see if they offer a similar service, and bear in mind that some packages may be cheaper with a user-cap, which may still be sufficient for family home use. The cheapest deals, however, are often governed by the length of the contract. Beware of being tied to a 12-18 month contract with a poor provider with no get-out clause.

Electronic subjects can cover almost anything that we're likely to buy from high street retailers so keep your eyes and ears open for anything that can produce a How-To article, such as problematic reception with broadband, getting to grips with a Smart-phone, etc – not to mention dealing with total shut down when the security system on the car won't let you in, no matter how much you try to persuade it that you *are* the legitimate owner!

Have you any cautionary tales to tell about electrical apparatus? Problems with service contracts? Obtaining efficient broadband in your area? Inadequate sales staff? Indecipherable instruction manuals?

Marketplace

Consumer pieces are always popular, especially if they contain cautionary tales about contracts and 'get-out clauses'. Letters pages are a good place to start, and so are the online How-To sites that are always keen to offer warnings to would-be customers and consumers. Located between two mountain ranges, the problems we've had with installing broadband would provide a weekly column for a year – if I wasn't so heartily sick of the subject. We have an indoor aerial, a booster, a modem and an outdoor aerial and still the thing only works on a 'will it, won't it' basis – often disconnecting right in the middle of an online banking session!

Build your Portfolio

Remember that we are aiming at building up a personal portfolio of How-To pieces, so no matter how modest, it all adds to our credentials as a serious non-fiction writer.

Another point to remember is that there is an article behind *everything* you encounter during your daily routine – no matter how mundane and/or familiar something is, there are countless different angles from which to view it and write a How-To about it.

Exercise 5: Computers

Everyone has something to say about computers – even if it's only 'how to exist without one'. I dare say that most of us have stories that have made us laugh, cry, tear out our hair, and driven us to contemplate murder – and we will not be alone. We might not be computer experts but we can qualify as computer-idiots and have something to say on the subject – even if it's how not to ...

Exercise 6: Electronics

Similarly *everyone* has experienced some problem caused by the 'electronic age' – there was the old joke about the only good reason having grandchildren was so they could programme the television recorder but we have to fend for ourselves in these days of HD stuff. Mobile phones have become so complicated (sophisticated?) that the selling point isn't whether the bloody thing functions as a *telephone* but whether it can make the tea or boil an egg in under 3 minutes - and costs in the region of £200-£500 quid into the bargain! How to choose ... or how not to choose.

Chapter Five

Culture & Society

This genre is the most broad-based of all because here the Self-Help and Self-Improvement books and articles can be marketed under a whole umbrella of different publications. In this context we are looking at 'culture' in terms of identity - of people who live in today's multi-cultural society' – and 'society' as acceptable social behaviour within that community. My first How-To book was *Exploring Spirituality*, which examined the problems caused by people wanting to break away from their established religious background (culture) and explore other alternative beliefs. My second and third, *The Good Divorce Guide* and *WLTM: The Dating Game* offered social comments, or Self-Help within a How-To context.

Culture

Our cultural background explains who we are and where we come from – and more often than not, in today's world – it explains where we are going. In recent years there has been a rapidly growing shift towards a greater diversity of cultures within the community, and there is always room for books and articles helping to banish the misunderstandings that often evolve when different cultures collide. A knowledge *and* understanding of different cultural backgrounds can produce a wide range of articles for an even wider range of outlets.

Culture also encompasses the growing Western trend for pagan and Wiccan beliefs, so much so, that much of what was once 'occult' is now considered mainstream. In fact, Wicca is said to be the fastest growing religion in the West and there is a wide band of publications and publishers catering for this new trend in spirituality. Bear in mind that this subject often overlaps the

MB&S (Mind, Body and Spirit) market and surprisingly, a UK How-To website, accepted the following:

How To Find Out More About Pagan Belief

Paganism is an umbrella term for the fastest growing belief in the Western world. In many people's minds, this trend has sinister undertones and they become concerned for children and family members who profess to be following what is often termed as an alternative religion. But what exactly is paganism, and how can we discover more about it?

- Firstly, it is necessary to define what pagans are not, as well as what they are. Pagans are not sexual deviants, do not worship the devil, are not evil, do not practice 'black magic' and do not harm people or animals in their rites.
- Paganism describes a group of contemporary or revivalist religions based on a reverence for Nature, and draws on the traditional religions of indigenous people throughout the world.
- Paganism encompasses a diverse community including Wiccans, Druids and Northern (Norse) traditions. Some groups concentrate on specific traditions or practices such as shamanism, earth mysteries, witchcraft or revivalist Celtic traditions.
- The majority of pagans share an ecological commitment that comes from the belief in the spirituality of the natural world.
- Although the Pagan Federation of Great Britain has no precise figures, in 2002 it estimated that the number of pagans in the British Isles was between 50,000 and 200,000.

Conclusion

Anyone wanting to know more about paganism can contact The Pagan Federation who are only too willing to allay any fears or misapprehension parents or teachers may have about a teenager's interest in the subject. Founded in 1971 The Pagan Federation now has affiliations all around the world, and ensures that pagans have the same rights as the followers of other beliefs and religions, and aims to provide information on pagan belief to the media, official bodies and the public community.

When writing about cultural matters not our own, it is essential that the content is dealt with sympathetically. Nevertheless, the West has always been fascinated by the East and there is plenty of scope within the Mind, Body & Spirit genre for articles on all manner of subjects, not to mention home-grown folklore and seasonal customs for the more mainstream publications. Have a look at Philip Gold's *Yom Kippur Party Goods*; Myron Jones's *Hey, Holy Spirit, It's Me Again*; Mélusine Draco's Traditional Witchcraft series; Siri Kirpal Kaur Khalso's *Sikh Spiritual Practice*; Aidan Rankin's *Shinto: a Celebration of Life*; Luke Eastwood's *The Druid's Primer* or Maggie Whitehouse's *Kabbalah Made Easy* for inspiration.

We live in a multi-cultural society so what interesting hints or How-To advice can you offer? Do you have any knowledge of alternative remedies, folk medicine, Eastern therapy, etc? Have you any advice on How-To cope with any problems or difficulties arising from alternative beliefs? What about your own home-grown customs and folklore?

Marketplace

Your first port of call is your local newsagent to see what's on offer for the MB&S writer. There are now dozens of magazines devoted solely to this genre, and the editor will be on the lookout for well-written pieces that examine the spirituality of alternative cultures. Publications catering for the more metaphysical aspects are usually subscription only, but do bear in mind that what 10 years ago would have been considered 'alternative' is now mainstream in this genre. Culture, however, isn't all about spirituality – it also covers philosophy, politics, folklore, customs, arts and entertainment, which *will* appeal to more mainstream editors if you can find an original slant on the How-To angle.

Society

Here we can also write about such a multitude of subjects that the list is endless – from 'how to organise charity events', or protect yourself against crime - to Self-Help is coping with all manner of personal problems, together with wide areas of Self-Improvement. The dictionary definition of Society is: *the conventions and opinions of a community; the fashionable world,* and so we can see just how much we have to draw from and offer our How-To advice. This piece of frivolity was a regular event in my home town and inspired a piece for the UK How-To site Howopia ...

How To Serve Afternoon Tea as a Fund Raiser

Few of us have time to stop in the middle of the afternoon for a leisurely tea, but the tradition can be revived in the form of a modest fund-raiser. Everyone enjoys a moment of self-indulgence and this idea can make use of somebody's attractive home – or even the village/church hall – for the occasion. You will need a team of 'ladies who bake' and to provide the china and linen to make it a success.

You will need:

Pretty tablecloths and napkins
China cups and saucers
Teaspoons and cake forks
Cake plates and paper doilies
Assortment of cakes and sandwiches
Large trays

- The venue needs to be accessible to cater for drop-in customers and casual passers-by on an afternoon when there is usually a lot of people about, i.e. Saturdays or market day. In summer it could be a garden tea party at someone's home.

- Publicise the event in the local free papers and on local radio (stating the purpose of the fund raising) and make a large poster/blackboard to stand outside attracting customers stating: 'Afternoon tea with home made cakes' or 'Delicious cream teas' and a set price per head. Have some leaflets prepared as hand-outs.

- If your volunteers are willing, you could also include a cake stall to tempt customers and when in season, add home-made jams and preserves.

- The type of tea to serve is a matter of personal taste but it is a good idea to offer a choice of Indian or China tea, Earl Grey or Lapsang Souchong, with an option of milk or lemon.

- Set individual tables for four people with a pretty cloth. Use paper ones if necessary but linen always looks nicer – and provide plenty of throw-away.

- Offer your customers a choice of, say, four sandwiches (one normal sized sandwich cut into quarters), and two portions of cake for a set price, with as much tea as they can drink. Don't charge for a refill as it look parsimonious, even if it is a fund raiser.

- Place four cups and saucers on the table and make the tea in the kitchen, using proper china teapots. Milk, sugar and lemon slices should be placed on the table. It doesn't matter if the designs and patterns don't match – as long as the cups and saucers do.

- Clear the dirty china immediately anyone leaves, and reset with clean. People don't want to sit down to a messy table, so change the table cloth if it becomes dirty.

- Try to keep the gathering intimate by having fewer rather

than a large number of tables. If the tables are set too far apart it will look unwelcoming. Have gentle music playing in the background and provide a small vase or bowl of flowers on each table.

- Allocate each volunteer a job – serving tea, serving cakes and sandwiches, clearing away, washing up, etc.

Conclusion

Village and church halls have always been used for local social events and will probably have all the necessary chairs and tables – there will also be an element of nostalgia for local people. This kind of event seldom makes lots of money but it provides a pleasant afternoon interlude and another community activity. If it is a run-away success, it can always be repeated or alternatively, host a coffee morning.

This, obviously, is a very English sort of event, but no matter where you live in the world, each culture has its own individual traditions – such as Bronwen and Frans Steine's *Japanese Art of Reiki* or Charlotte Carnegie's *The Incomplete Guide to Yoga*, both subjects now completely integrated into Western society. In fact, any social activity falls into this category and the editorial doors should be wide open for your 'How-to …'

What family or local traditions can you advise people how to do? What about self-protection in urban streets? Or ideas for Self-Help and Self-Improvement? What sort of social activities take place in your area? How can you join in …?

Marketplace

I often incorporate traditional country How-To's in articles for *The Countryman*, which are largely bits and pieces handed down through the family for generations. This is a sneaky creative writing technique of blending contemporary living with old-fashioned household hints, tips and recipes to give an article a much wider appeal. Plenty of scope for 'how to feel better about yourself' articles and on the full-length front, there are also countless ideas for Self-Help and Self-Improvement. For example: Suki Pryce's *Do We Need To Be So Screwed Up?!*; John C Robinson's *Three Stages of Aging*; or Melanie Chan's *Life Coaching – Life Changing*.

Build Your Portfolio

Bear in mind that you are unique and that no one can have access to the same experiences – which means you have the ability to generate unique responses to a situation and produce a fresh slant for an article. We all have dozens of social niceties that can be modernised for the How-To market, we just have to find that original approach that will appeal to an editor.

Exercise 7: Culture

Personal experience, light-hearted observation or information-based articles can advise people how to cope with problems/difficulties arising from culture-clashes. Even the rural-urban viewpoint can encounter severe culture-shocks as my own *Signposts For Country Living* revealed. Study this section and produce a short seasonal How-To piece – even if it's only for the parish magazine or local free paper.

Exercise 8: Society

Again we have an extremely diverse category and the target market is virtually every magazine, newspaper or online How-To site in the English-speaking world! The right approach for each individual editor is still essential but any writer should be able to produce a reasonable How-To piece to fit into this slot. Which element of contemporary society, for example, would you send to your own personal *Room 101*? And how could the situation be rectified?

Chapter Six

Education

An emotive subject and one that is never out of the news these days because the subject of education affects everyone – not just teaching staff. From pre-school to obtaining a university degree, pupils, parents, grandparents and family friends all become embroiled in the lengthy progress. Even Jamie Oliver had something to say on the matter of school meals, and turned his ideas into a book and television series both in the UK and America. The weekend broadsheets often have a separate supplement for education, and check out the financial supplement for How-To articles on student loans and finances.

Writers don't necessarily have to have their own children to find some How-To advice to impart. I encountered the following aspect of higher education having been asked to read the completed offering of a friend's son – and had to do some quick research to find out exactly what the personal statement needed to achieve. Thankfully the Internet and the *Daily Telegraph's* educational supplement came to the rescue to provide the necessary background material ... and you'll notice credit has been given where appropriate.

How To Write A Personal Statement

Basically, a personal statement allows you to set out your reasons for applying for a particular university course, and convince the admissions tutors to offer you a place. In 4000 words you need to stand out from the thousands of would-be students vying for places, sometimes at a ratio of 20.1. Richard Cairns, Headmaster of Brighton College, writing in the *Daily Telegraph's* Education section, described it as a vital part of the university's application process, and pointed out that although your academic grades will catch an admission tutor's eye, it will be a well-constructed personal statement that "convinces them of your motivation, potential and ability for further study".

- This will be your only opportunity to demonstrate a genuine interest in, and a passion for, your chosen subject – but do avoid using terms like 'passion' and 'life-changing experiences'. In fact, avoid clichéd statements and do not pepper the text with superlatives that merely sound contrived.
- Aim to explain three key ideas: why you want to study a particular course; why you will excel at that particular course; and how your other interests will support and complement your studies.
- For practical science course such as medicine, veterinary, physics, engineering, you need to convince tutors that you fully understand what your chosen career entails in practice as well as theory.
- For the less practical courses, Richard Cairns advises that the emphasis must be on proving that your intellectual curiosity extends beyond the A-level syllabus by discussing "which scientific breakthroughs or seminal contributions to a particular field have intrigued and challenged you".
- If applying for a joint course of two separate disciplines (i.e. modern languages and philosophy), you will need to explain why you wish to study both subjects and how they relate to each other.
- Before beginning to write your personal statement, set out a clear structure and make a list of important bullet points that will need to be included. For example: begin with a strong opening statement or 'hook' explaining why you wish to study a particular course. This should be followed by two to three paragraphs providing evidence of your

aptitude and enthusiasm for study. The last sections should be used briefly for extra-curricular interests – and finally, a "concise summary of your motivation and potential".

- Support your claims with precise examples of books and articles you have read, and details of any relevant work experience. "And make sure you have actually done everything mentioned in the personal statement or you might come unstuck if you are called in for an interview."

- There are hundreds of books and websites offering examples/templates for a personal statement, but this will only make yours one of a thousand simple versions. A natural, original statement will be far more effective than a standardised version – and don't copy other people's ideas.

- Don't leave all this to the last minute and be prepared to spend a lot of time, thinking, writing, re-thinking and re-writing. Ask teachers for advice, since they will be required to write a reference supporting your application – and they should be able to pick up on any errors or howlers!

- Check spelling, grammar and punctuation by getting someone responsible and/or experienced to read through for continuity and omissions.

Conclusion

As Richard Cairns also pointed out, "it is impossible to overestimate the importance of writing a clear and convincing personal statement". More than 99% of the 55,000 courses available in UK universities no longer require potential students to take an aptitude test, or attend for an interview, and the personal statement is the only application the admission tutor will see in order to make a decision. Be inventive – be original!

Tips

Although extra-curricular activities are of interest keep the information to a minimum - see Durham University's check-list for the criteria it uses for assessing applications. Keep within the limit of 4,000 words and resist the urge to be whimsical or amusing.

Warning

UCAS runs applications through anti-plagiarism software and if your is discovered to be a copy, the application will be voided.

As we can see, writing a personal statement involved a lot more than just cobbling together a nice little essay, since this has evolved into a highly complex procedure. It took a lot of research but at the end of the day, the information gathered from different sources produced quite a lengthy but informative How-To piece. The research also turned up other subjects that could be used to create other pieces such as: 'how to manage student finances', 'how to find out about studying abroad to avoid student fees', 'how-to obtain student travel discounts, student insurance', etc.

What are friends telling you about their children's problems with education? This can range from 'how to choose the right pre-school group' to 'how to choose the right university'. Are your children involved in a school-garden scheme – and has it changed their view of 'greens' they've grown themselves? What about packed lunches? School dinners? The cost of a uniform?

Marketplace

Any publication that features educational subjects – from the regular broadsheet supplements to women's magazines and local 'back to school' features in the local paper all offer publishing opportunities. Thinking outside the box on this one helps because your How-To advice doesn't have to be about the education system – anything that helps mums to provide healthy packed lunches, or find good deals on second-hand uniforms will be of interest. Check out the education supplements for changing trends that can be adapted into mini How-To hints and tips and look at the parenting magazines for market outlets. There are even eBay sites and swap shops for bargain school uniforms – how do we go about finding out where they are? If writing from personal experience, then there is a niche for full-length educational books of all types and for all age groups.

Build Your Portfolio

Educational also covers further education for adults so contact your local college and see what's on offer … and then tell the local readership how to join!

Exercise 9: Education

If you don't have children of your own, eavesdrop and pinch ideas from conversations overheard on the train or bus – or filch information from friends with children of different age groups. Bear in mind that most 'educational' features tend to be seasonal and coincide with the build-up to the start of term time – so plan ahead. As a footnote, I was recently asked for my own 'personal statement' when applying to an online site for freelance journalism – even with my age and experience I wouldn't have had a clue except for the fact that I'd recently found out about it and written the above! We're never too old to learn.

Chapter Seven

Fashion & Style

Fashion and style are very much personal things and most of what we see as *haute couture* is far removed from what others would call 'high street' fashion. In this category, how to dress tips for hundreds of different social occasions would be just as marketable as how not to dress hints. Our dress sense speaks volumes about us and unless we're complete extroverts, conforming is usually what the average person wants to do. Although I once worked in the 'posh end' of the rag-trade in London in the 1970s, one tip for example, aimed at the would-be joiner of the field-sports fraternity is more in my line: 'How to Age a New Barbour'. Put it in the dog's bed for a month before wearing it in public, since no self-respecting country person would be seen dead wearing a new one!

Fashion
How-To fashion tips should be aimed at the age-group reading the magazine or newspaper. Teens and Twenties might be interested in 'how to arrange a swaps party' where a group of friends bring their unwanted clothes, shoes, bags, make-up, CDs etc and exchange things amongst themselves. Popular fashion tips on how to re-vamp an old outfit by the clever use of accessories, will often tempt an editor. The following How-To, for example, was kept short and sweet but it found its way onto an online website.

How To Turn the Old Fashioned Brooch Into a Modern Fashion Accessory
The Queen's Diamond Jubilee put the brooch firmly back in the spotlight as a fashion accessory, but how can the lesser-monied utilise the contents of Granny's jewellery box?

- Brooches don't have to be worn on a lapel – although they are useful for livening up a previous season's dress or coat.
- Brooches can be worn at the hips and waists of trousers, attached to belts, or added to chokers, hair bands, hats and evening bags.
- Create your own ideas: Balmain caused a sensation in *Vogue* magazine by fastening folded handkerchiefs with diamond brooches and turning them into bracelets.
- Celtic design pins and brooches can add a new dimension to scarves, throws and pashminas.

Conclusion:

If you haven't inherited any family pieces, 'costume-jewellery' can be just as effective. Look for interesting brooches on eBay and at car boot sales.

Fashion appears regularly in magazines and television programmes and there's even a regular prize for the Best Dressed at racecourse Ladies' Days. Many of the stunning outfits are vintage 1950s – and this suggests other 'how to dress' for other occasions. Although we might not like to admit it, there *is* a 'dress code' for almost all social, family and business occasions – and if you need more proof just look at how the 'fashion police' lambast the celebrities in the media for any perceived fashion 'goof'. On a more mundane level, we might offer how not to dress for your spouse's annual company 'do'.

We've all seen fashion come and go, so have you any useful How-To tips about utilising the contents of a wardrobe to produce something new and exciting? Or how to care for the Jimmy Choos my other half bought me for a Christmas present one year!

Marketplace

Every teenage or women's magazine carries fashion pages, and so do most newspapers – even local free papers. The secret here is pitching for the right age group or social set – especially ideas such as 'how to pack for a carry-on luggage only holiday' or 'how to travel light'. This sort of proposal is often seasonal, so think about pitching your ideas 6-12 months ahead. If you have young daughters then think about money-saving How-To's for the tweenie magazines.

Style

Style and fashion aren't always the same thing – and style is very much a personal taste. It is quite possible to be stylish without being the least bit fashionable. The dictionary says of style: *the distinctive manner peculiar to an individual especially when considered superior or desirable; imposingly smart.* How-To tips in this category should be aimed at encouraging the reader to improve their own appearance, rather than going for a fashionable image, which never takes into account age, height, weight or shape! This How-To piece went back to basics:

How To Give Yourself A Make Over

There often comes a time when we decide that we need a change of image. It may be because of the breakdown of a long-term relationship, a career change, or just because we want to introduce the feel-good factor back into our lives. To begin: take the cross-gender mirror test – and be honest. Whether you are male or female, take all your clothes off and stand in front of a full-length mirror. What do you see?

- **Are you overweight?** We all put on a little bit as we get older and our metabolism changes but if there's a mass of flab and sagging extremities, ask yourself whether you'd fancy you, if you were a wo/man? Is it a result of over-indulgence and a lack of self-control; or do you need to face up to dealing with health problems? Make a doctor's appointment and get yourself checked out – then start looking at ways to rid yourself of the excess pounds. Take up swimming, walking or running and start to feel better about yourself, especially if you're meeting a new circle of friends.

- **Does your hairstyle need attention?** A change of hairstyle can do wonders for low self-esteem and can, in some circumstances, alter the whole way we feel about ourselves and life in general. Women, in particular recognise the importance of the drastic new hairstyle when life is at a low point – so go mad and do something about it. The long hair versus. 40-plus arguments always cite the glamorous celebrities, but we must accept that they have the finances to ensure they keep looking good – the rest of us aren't so fortunate. Long hair can be extremely ageing, for both men and women on the wrong side of 45. So whether it's a drastic new cut or colour, go for something different – unkempt hair does nothing for anyone.
- **Is your personal hygiene up to standard?** This isn't a question of do you smell? It's more a general assessment of whether you still pay attention to keeping hands and fingernails looking nice. Do you regularly remove body hair and keep your underwear in good repair?
- **Is your appearance outdated?** Women should be realistic about wearing skirts too short for their age. There are quite a number of 'ladies of a certain age' who still enjoy wearing 'tarty-trotters', i.e. 4-inch stiletto heels, because they feel smarter when going somewhere special, but the combination of short skirts *and* high heels, however, is best left to the 20-30-somethings, with elegance being the province of the older woman. Alternatively, are you still clinging to the Earth Mother regalia, or squeezing yourself into straight-

leg jeans and black leather as the Big 50 looms closer? Is your age or shape conducive to wearing skimpy tops and shorts to the supermarket?

- Men should consider whether their beard makes them look much older than their true age? Perhaps a re-styling would make a tremendous change to your appearance. Although the tide is beginning to turn and men are being seen more and more out in the shopping malls, older males are not always known for their sartorial elegance. Is it time for you to abandon the 'medallion man' image in favour of something smarter? Remember that an out-dated appearance gives the impression of someone clinging onto lost youth.

- So now is the time to opt for a total reinvention of yourself and head for Weightwatchers, or the local gym and start to shed those excess pounds. Don't be afraid to ask for help or advice – experienced fitness professionals will be able to help with the best diet or training programme for your age, build or state of health. Weightwatchers can still help you to lose weight online, even if there are no meetings in your area.

- Do change your hairstyle and if you've been a devotee of Gothic black, it may be the right time to consider a change of colour, too. Invest in one of the monthly style magazines aimed at the hairdressing fraternity (or borrow from a hairdressing chum) that gives modern styles for every length of hair for both men and women of all ages.

- Review your wardrobe with a critical eye. Look at the adverts in the weekend colour supplements and see what's in fashion among the celebrities in your age group. Remember that they spend pounds on personal shoppers and trainers, but you can copy ideas that have cost them a fortune. You don't have to throw everything away, just team up different items and jazz them up with colourful accessories.

- When you have money to spare, have a look at the designer clothes on sale on eBay. For a fraction of the cost of a new coat, you can buy a whole outfit that has hardly been worn (including shoes and handbag), and if you haven't paid full price for it, then you won't be so paranoid about wearing designer clothes every day – it all helps contribute to the change of image. But don't be fooled into wearing something that doesn't suit you just because it's in fashion!
- Metabolism can also alter the smell of favourite perfumes, colognes, etc., so make sure that you're not clinging to an overpowering fragrance that, combined with the natural acids in your skin, may suggest paint stripper. A new perfume or cologne can be almost as satisfying as a new hairstyle, but choose wisely. Make up also needs to be toned down as we get older, so ask your local beauty representatives for help – and maybe get some free samples.

Conclusion

A personal make over doesn't need the resources of Trinny and Susannah, or Gok Wan [UK style gurus] but we can learn from their experiments. The gimmick for their shows is to make the less than perfect figure appear stylish – and helps to avoid the mutton dressed as lamb look.

We've all had the occasional disaster in wearing the wrong outfit, and left with the feeling of being over- or under-dressed. And as we get older, we've all had the moment of enlightenment when we have a flash of insight that tells us we no longer look good in … tight jeans, low-cut dresses, black leather, vivid colours, Gothic black … the list can be endless and all down to the individual's perception of *themselves*. It's often a fact that's overlooked, that as we get older, the younger we dress – the older we look. My mother always said never to wear white next to the skin, or black leather after you've turned forty and she was a *very* stylish lady.

Have you any personal How-To tips for developing a personal style? Can you draw on the experiences of friends and family? How many How-To hints can you offer? How did you make the age transformation?

Marketplace

Again, every female publication is a potential marketplace for 'how to acquire style' – and quite a few of the male magazines, too. These markets are also strictly age-group orientated, so plenty of market research before submitting. Don't forget to consider the sporting magazines for pitching style ideas. Often local papers and regional magazines run seasonal fashion/style features so try to get a foot in the door with an 'advertorial' featuring local shops. And don't forget you can pick up the most stylish, designer outfits off eBay for a fraction of the original cost. I went to a wedding with a friend with both of us dressed in comparable designer outfits – hers cost in excess of £500 new while mine was an eBay purchase for under £20 … And have a look a Jules Standish's *How Not To Wear Black*, as an example of how to write a full-length book on the subject.

Build Your Portfolio

Spend a lot of time looking at the fashion pages in magazines and newspapers, so that you are fully aware of what individual editors are looking for – and know what's currently in fashion as far as colours and textures are concerned. I was recently contemplating getting rid of a very expensive woollen jumper that had taken on the 'skinny' look through repeated washings. Then I read a fashion piece about 'trophy jumpers' that cost in the region of £500-£1200 and the photos showed a garment almost identical to the one I was thinking of throwing out! And don't forget hair-styling publications, too – study these the next time you go to the hairdresser – and remember you don't have to be an experienced stylist to pick up handy How-To hints for keeping hair healthy.

Exercise 10: Fashion

Simple How-To tips are always best suited to 'fillers' and readers' letters, although online How-To websites are always worth looking at. Even if your contribution is only how to make make-up and toiletries last longer – we all have our little economies that we can share with others, so add these to your portfolio. I once got away with 'how to get the best value out of a toilet roll'!

Exercise 11: Style

In its broadest sense, this can refer to personal style as well as life-style How-To hints. Most 'how to dress' and 'how to behave' for interviews, social events and appointments would probably appeal to most editors of women's magazines – and even some **Business** magazines. We're not talking about glam events like the school prom or Ascot – we're looking at parent-teacher meetings, job interviews and court hearings. For the latter, a friend of mine who'd done this several times, recommends shabby-chic as it shows that you're used to better things but you're desperately trying to manage on the pittance of a maintenance allowance!

Chapter Eight

Food & Drink

This is probably the most over-subscribed category in How-To writing, so your proposal is going to have to be something really special – or different. The world's media is obsessed with the subject and from anorexia to obesity, the genre caters for every palette, food fad and household budget. As I've observed in *Life-Writes*, old-fashioned remedies, recipes and household hints are popular with editors but they need an unusual or unexpected spin to bring them up to date. I've had how to make WWII recipes as an accompaniment to a WWII evening accepted for publication; not to mention reminders of how to make those 'home from school' teas of bubble and squeak, cheese and potato pie, and eggy-bread – which would probably give the 'food police' heart failure.

Food

As with all How-To articles, the odd anecdote thrown in for good measure never goes amiss. I often use *Food & Feast in Medieval England* by Peter Hammond (Sutton) and *Food in the Ancient World* by John M Wilkins and Shaun Hill (Blackwell) to spice up the text. And my recollection of the best breakfast I've ever had using leftovers was when working in Edinburgh as a conference organiser. It was an early-morning call and while the others ploughed their way through fruit, toast and black coffee, I had a huge plate of fried leftover haggis and potatoes courtesy of the hotel chef – and it's still the best breakfast I've ever eaten at six o' clock in the morning! Which leads us to …

How To Use Leftovers, or the Art of Using Up

When food or money was scarce, especially during the war years, every scrap of food would have been saved. Some of these economical little hints have been passed on as part of a family's tradition, being handed down over the years. And many can still come in handy when there's still a week to go before the salary is paid into the bank.

- Bacon fat: keep it for frying fish, meat, eggs, omelettes etc., Both lard and dripping contain palmitic and stearic fatty acids, important for energy metabolism and normal growth.
- Bones: boil to make into stock and gravy. Add lots of vegetables to the stock for a supply of nourishing soup.
- Cold sausages: slice and add to potato salad or mash; season and use as a filling for sandwiches or jacket potatoes.
- Ends of cheese: grate and mix with an equal quantity of freshly grated cheese and use as required in any cooked dish, Welsh rarebit, jacket potatoes, etc.
- Stale bread: crisp in the oven and crush with a rolling pin; use as a coating for fish, croquettes, cutlets, etc., and as a topping for cottage pie.
- Rasher of bacon: a single rasher of bacon can be served with slices of peeled apple; left-over mashed potato, or sliced boiled potato fried in bacon fat.
- Finally chop a slice of bacon or cold sausage, fry and sprinkle over scrambled egg on toast; or add to the scrambled egg as it begins to thicken.
- Eggy bread: for a 'home from school' treat; beat an egg into a bowl and season. Cut a slice of bread in half and dip in the egg – fry in bacon fat.
- Cold, left-over vegetables can be used to garnish salads, thicken soups, or to add bulk to a cottage pie made from left-over roast meat.
- Fry left-over greens and mashed potato to make traditional 'bubble and squeak'.

Conclusion

As Mrs Beeton wrote: "Great care should be taken that nothing which might, by proper management, be turned to good account, is thrown away, or suffered to be wasted in the kitchen."

Regional food can also be served up to provide endless 'how to make' articles for both regional and national publications. Old family recipes, farmhouse cookery, wild food from the hedgerows, summer picnics, meals for students, comfort food ... the list is endless. And if you have enough material, there could be enough for a full-length book on the subject, although thorough market research is needed to make sure something similar isn't already in print. See how your favourite cookery writers present their 'how to cook' books – for example my favourite is Nigel Slater because his approach is non-precious and easy to follow and I would love his kitchen!

What are your favourite family recipes? Do you have any regional or seasonal recipes that have a special meaning? Can you provide simple, tasty How-To 'fillers' for magazines or local newspapers?

Marketplace

The next time you visit a large bookstore, take a look at the number and variety of cookery books on sale. Next consider the large number of women's magazines that feature a cookery page and study the depth of detail that goes into each piece. What about the endless number of sporting and hobbyist publications such as shooting, caravanning, sailing, canal boating, walking and camping – the editor of any of these might be interested in 'how to cater' for individual circumstances. If you have the experience, there's also the outlet for Self-Help features (or books) on diets, eating disorders, and other topics including titles such as Rachel Patterson's *Kitchen Witchcraft*, Dave Reavly's

Healthy Eating and Pollution Protection for Kids and Gwynne Davies' *Death on a Fork*.

Drink

Drink doesn't *necessarily* mean alcohol – there are all sorts of traditional beverages, fruit cordials and summer punches that fall into this category. Just like food, drink can also be evocative of times past – like grandma's homemade lemonade, or that first Pimm's tasted at a summer ball. Or drinking Charbonnel & Walker's hot chocolate by a roaring log fire. Then there's the darker side of the subject such as how to cope with alcoholism in teenagers and partners.

How To Make a Traditional Hot Irish Whiskey

No Irish winter sporting event would be complete without a hot whiskey – and certainly no one would be sacrilegious enough to attempt to use anything other than Paddy's or Jameson for the purpose. On the sidelines at the Gaelic football and hurling, on the coursing field, track or racecourse many of those present will be seen supping from those plastic cups ...

What you'll need:

One generous measure of Irish whiskey
Slice of lemon
4 whole cloves
Teaspoon of sugar
Hot water

- Pour the whiskey into a glass.
- Place a teaspoon in the glass and add the sugar, lemon, cloves and two measure of boiling water.
- Stir well, pressing the lemon to extract the juice – and drink.
- If serving your own mix at a sporting event use clear

glasses with the sugar, lemon and cloves already inside. Stack the glasses one inside the other until needed and to prevent spilling the ingredients. Just add whiskey and hot water – and serve immediately.

Conclusion:

There's an old Irish belief that this concoction can cure a broken heart. And if it doesn't work the first time, take ten of them in quick succession. From *The Feckin' Book of Irish Recipes.*

Drinking usually means companionship and parties – whether it's a champagne buffet at a friend's wedding, or a holiday cream tea with Earl Grey and fresh strawberries. What drink can you serve to be different for a children's party … or a Hallowe'en bash? Then there are the countless natural ingredients from the fields and hedgerows that can make the most lethal of homemade wines!

Do you have any interesting hints and How-To's that can make a family gathering go with a swing? Or how to put a new spin on an old concept such as a tired old 'cheese and wine' party, for example. Or how to make a non-alcoholic punch?

Marketplace

Whereas drink has a slightly more restricted marketplace than food, with a certain mental ingenuity and a stretch of the imagination, it is possible to come up with ideas that an editor would find appealing. My fund-raising tea party or coffee-morning suggestion (see **Culture & Society**) was snapped up by an online How-To site for publication, and could easily be adapted for a village fete or school parents' evening. Look at journals for the caring professions that might be interested in ideas for low-cost promotions. Countryside and 'mind, body and spirit' magazines would consider 'how to make wines and fruit drinks' from traditional recipes, providing the right slant is given to the article.

Build Your Portfolio

This category needn't be restricted to one idea, as the subject of food and drink seems to have a knock-on effect. In these days of austerity, some of the old WWII recipes could be adapted for modern use: 'how to make a bread and butter pudding' from stale bread, for example. Or 'how to bottle fruit' or 'how to make your own jam/pickles/chutney' after a pick-your-own excursion, or visit to a farmers' market.

Have a little tale to tell before adding the How-To suggestion as this gives more editor appeal. For example, our Welsh Sunday morning market was a social event as well as an opportunity to stock up on really fresh vegetables for Sunday lunch, and when we caught up with farming neighbours for a coffee, a natter and a *huge* breakfast roll of cold roast pork!

Exercise 12: Food

As Delia Smith has observed: "Nature is perfectly capable of providing us with a varied and interesting diet throughout the year, and by buying things in their natural season, you'll be getting them at their most plentiful and therefore at their cheapest."

For this exercise think in terms of seasonal ingredients and pitch your idea for several months down the line, such as the How-To tips for using up end of season green tomatoes, which could also fit into the **Gardening** category.

Exercise 13: Drink

And cookery writer Elizabeth David commented that if we "spent as much money on wine for cooking, as we do on stock cubes, gravy granules and instant stock, we would all enjoy better food". If you're not into wine then try dry cider as a How-

To hint – or any other alternative. Or have you any favourite pick-me-up beverages that you can share with a readership?

Chapter Nine

Friends & Family

This category is another wide reaching marketplace and can cover everything from 'how to arrange a simple birthday surprise' to 'how to cope with the loss of a loved one'. Friendship often comes with its own set of rules and not infrequently, its own set of problems – such as 'how to avoid a friend's boyfriend/husband' or even 'how to end a friendship'. Family matters are frequently complicated, and have spawned countless books on 'how to come to terms' with these difficulties, as demonstrated by Lynne Hackles in *Writing From Life: How to turn your person experience into profitable prose*, in which she shamelessly exploited her friends and family into the bargain!

Friends

The dictionary defines a 'friend' as a close or intimate acquaintance, and often we can be closer to an old school friend than we are to our family. In fact, E M Forster penned the sentiment that if faced with the choice between betraying his friend and his country, he hoped he would have the guts to betray his country. Friends are the only people for whom we can pick up a pebble on a beach and send it with a note "Saw this and thought of you" and they know why you've sent it. The following comes from Mélusine Draco's *Magic Crystals, Sacred Stones* …

How To Make a Good Luck Charm for a Friend

Most people have a 'lucky piece' that they carry with them for good luck, and it's a custom that's been going strong since the days of ancient Egypt. Today's charm (or amulet to give the correct name) can be in the form of a key fob, special good luck stone, a birth sign or a particular piece of jewellery… or something special we make ourselves.

What you'll need:

10 inches of 18-guage silver wire
Small stones or pebbles
Key rings
Small long-nosed pliers

- One of the most popular personal charms is a lucky stone that can be an unusual pebble we find by mere chance. To make an amulet you will need about 10 inches of 18-guage silver wire to wrap around the stone just as you would wrap a parcel - from side to side and from top to bottom.
- When you are sure the stone cannot fall out, create a loop at the top by winding the wire around a thin pencil. Weave the wire back through the cage and when it is secure, remove the pencil, leaving the loop open enough to thread through a key ring, piece of cord or neck chain.
- If you are lucky enough to find a tiny hagstone - a stone with a naturally bored hole through it and which is considered especially lucky - this can be prepared in the same way, or placed in a small pouch to be carried around in a handbag or briefcase.
- Personal charms are believed to offer protection against ill luck, accident and the 'evil eye' but need to symbolise something that suggests good luck to the recipient – perhaps a favourite plant, animal or bird. Sometimes, these images can be suggested by the texture or patterns in the stones.
- Alternatively, an appropriate 'bon voyage' card containing the feather of a swallow, or a 'good luck' card containing a four-leaf clover or shamrock can also be classed as a personal charm.
- Because the charm says 'I saw this and thought of you', it

automatically carries good wishes with it, even if neither the sender nor the recipient is of a superstitious nature.

Conclusion

Making a good luck charm for another person is the most meaningful token of love and friendship. The effort required in making a personalised charm adds its own degree of special comfort and protection. Friends or family members can exchange these simple keepsakes that will mean nothing to an outsider, but will be a treasured gift for the recipient. Keep your eyes open for small items that immediately bring a friend or relative to mind, especially if there is an anniversary, birthday or examination coming up.

Needless to say, any How-To piece on friendship must refrain from being judgemental or 'preachy' regardless of the age group it's aimed at. Friendship is a very precious – or dangerous – thing and needs to be handled with care. My childhood friend always sends me birthday cards illustrated with bluebell woods as it speaks volumes to both of us, and I chose a bluebell wood for one of my covers, because the book had also been dedicated to her.

What experiences have you had relating to friendship? Have you a life-long friend who has inspired or exasperated you? How do you cope when one of you 'moves on'?

Marketplace

This target market is probably more suited to the women's monthly glossy mags with more of an in-depth, psychological slant to your How-To advice. Although if you're going down the road of 'how to cope with your best friend running off with your prize marrow', then it could be better suited to the weekly publications. Teenage magazines often feature problems relating to friendship and if you have children of your own, then it's possible you can also relate to this age-group.

Family

One of the most popular family-oriented subjects is constructing a family-tree, or researching into the history of our ancestors along the lines of the popular television genealogy programme *Who Do You Think You Are?* – with plenty of How-To advice on 'how to get started'. We currently have a project going that will be presented to my partner's grandson on his eighteenth birthday in four years' time – since we've already discovered that his great-great-grandfather was hung by the British in Cork gaol, it may make for some interesting, if not embarrassing reading!

The subject of finding a suitable care home for an elderly relative, however, came about as a result of 85-year old Uncle Sean finally admitting he was finding it becoming increasingly more and more difficult to look after himself. The following How-To was a result of the investigations into finding the right sort of accommodation for someone who was still remarkably fit, but whose mind was starting to wander. In addition there was the problem of his ageing terrier to take into account.

How To Find The Right Care Home

With people living longer it is inevitable that many more will have to give up their homes and move into a residential care home. Whether you are considering the option for yourself, or facing the prospect of putting a member of the family into care, the first step is knowing where to look for the right information.

- Firstly, log on to the Care Quality Commission's website where you can read a brief description and inspection reports for every care home in the UK.
- Contact your local council for an assessment to see whether you (or your loved one) qualifies for support with fees. If the reason for residential care is medical, you may

qualify for full-funding by the NHS, which carries out its own assessment. If nursing care is required make sure there is a registered nurse on duty 24/7.

- Ask around people you know and find out which homes have the best reputation. Make sure you visit two or three that have vacancies – and don't be afraid to drop in unannounced.
- Ask for a full tour and take the time to talk to both staff and residents – and don't be afraid to ask questions. Ask to see the menus for the past few days and make sure they serve the food you or your loved one likes. The home may even invite you to lunch with the residents so you can judge for yourself.
- Check whether you will be allowed to put your own possessions in your room (i.e. personal TV and radio); if you can make your own decisions about what to wear, and what time you go to bed. Are you allowed outside whenever you like. Are there gardens, sun-lounge, etc.
- Remaining active is beneficial for both physical and mental health. Ask if the home encourages exercise and organises other leisure/social activities.
- Make sure you fully understand the fees and make sure you request a list of any 'extra' for which you will be charged on top of the weekly rate.
- Take into account that most residential care homes will not allow residents to have pets. If you are unable to take your pet with you there are animal charities such as Dogs Trust, Blue Cross and Wood Green who will be able to look after your pet, or find them a new home.

Conclusion

Make your enquiries well in advance, after all, a care home provides the two main reasons why you are unable to manage for yourself – the need for care and a home. It also gives ample time to find a suitable place that will allow you to take your pet if you cannot bear to be separated.

This type of How-To article needs to contain as much information as possible, with plenty of hints, tips and side bars giving contacts and websites. Family problems, however, make up a large proportion of magazine and newspaper content and often provide the first steps for others in obtaining help, or consulting the right people about health, social or welfare issues. Research your project well! Family issues also involve the pleasanter aspects such as family parties, anniversaries and get-togethers – but they don't generate as much editor-interest!

How-To's on family issues come better from someone who writes from personal experience - whether as a family member, or close family friend. Has anyone you know personally been involved in a divorce, suicide, bankruptcy, financial scandal – or any other issue that has caused serious problems for the family?

Marketplace

Get the subject and approach right and most of us can produce a competent How-To piece relating to our family that would be suitable for the wide range of women's publications - not to mention those specialising in children, parenting, health care, psychology, 'mind, body and spirit', etc. The subject matter ranges from 'how to arrange simple family get-togethers' (i.e. christenings) to 'how to avoid inter-family squabbles over wedding plans', or coping with sibling rape, murder and divorce. Lots of light-hearted stuff to choose from as well, but the more serious the subject, the more in-depth your writing needs to be. Nevertheless, this subject probably offers the widest range of opportunities for full-length books on Self-Help and Improvement: such as Phil Jourdan's *Praise of Motherhood*, Dan

Cohen-Sherbok's *What Do You Do When Your Parents Live Forever;*
Kimerer L LaMothe's *Family Planting.*

Build Your Portfolio

The larger your family and circle of friends, the easier it will be
to draw on material suitable for How-To hints and articles. The
best I could come up with was a simple good luck charm for a
very special, long-term friend but perhaps you can think of more
enterprising ideas – perhaps friendship is too personal to share.
On the family front, what with the feuding of *his* family, and the
amazing characters in mine, I can work this vein of experience for
years.

Friends: Exercise 14

Surprisingly, this exercise turned out to be the most difficult of all
in terms of producing a simple How-To on the subject of
friendship. Suggestions on 'how to make new friends' (see
Entertainment) might offer a solution, but I really struggled to
find something I *wanted* to write about.

Family: Exercise 15

By comparison the category of '**Family** offers so much How-To
material that we have our pick of topics that would be of interest
to an editor from 'how to make a family occasion speech' to 'how
to re-home the family dog' (see **Pets**). If we think about it, every
single member of the (extended) family across the age-divide
could probably each provide one How-To piece. From baby-
toddler How-To's to dealing with cantankerous grandparents
and great-aunts, each one can provide a How-To cameo for publication.

Chapter Ten

Games & Pastimes

Games and pastimes can be aimed at adults as well as children – and there are hundreds of traditional games that can be updated to bring fun to any form of organised or family entertainment. A simple How-To hint to encourage everyone to participate is to play as a team – this means that the least gifted can still be part of the winning side. We used this game-plan to play *Trivial Pursuit* at Christmas so that grandparents and small children could be included – even if they didn't actually participate – and it didn't matter how we divided everyone up, the oldies always won! Pastimes generally refer to hobbies and/or collecting, and the opportunities for How-To articles is endless, since nearly every form of hobby and pastime will have a magazine or newsletter, of varying levels of expertise, pertaining to it.

Games

Games are defined in the dictionary as: *a competitive amusement according to a system of rules*, which allow the participants to use teamwork and/or personal skill in order to be declared the winner; activities such as chess, darts and snooker come under the heading of games. Lots of old-fashioned games can be adapted for modern use and included in local fund-raising activities. For example: one of the most enduring of traditional games is …

How To Bob For Apples

Bobbing for apples, is a game often played in connection with Hallowe'en, by filling a tub or a large basin with water and putting apples in the water. Because apples are less dense than water, they float at the surface. In Scotland, this is called 'dooking', i.e. ducking, and in Ireland it is known as 'Snap Apple'.

- Players (individuals or team-members) try to catch an apple with their teeth.
- The use of hands is not allowed, and often tied behind the back to prevent cheating.
- The game is best played outdoors as there is a tremendous amount of water splashed about. So provide plenty of towels.
- This game can be included in harvest festivals, village fetes, bonfire nights or Hallowe'en parties for both children and adults.

Conclusion

Because of the nature of the game and the fact that all the players have to dunk their heads into the water, public occasions might have to bow to Health & Safety and use the alternative method of hanging the apples on a string, and keep the ducking tub for home use only.

Sometimes it can be easy to introduce traditional games to community events if a modern twist is added. For example: one traditional garden fete regular was 'bowling for the pig' – a knockout game of skittles where the winner was awarded a live piglet donated by a local farmer. Over the years the prize was adapted and the winner received their prize from the local butcher, all prepared for the freezer. The modern version could offer prizes of different sized china piggy-banks, ornaments or toy pigs that would encourage children to take part and offer more than one prize to add to the fun.

How many traditional games can you think of, that could provide modern entertainment? Can any of them be turned

into How-To ideas for potential publication? Or fund-raising ideas?

Marketplace

Any magazines that cater for children or children's entertainment; or even possibly care professionals' journals where the elderly would also remember 'parlour games' from their childhood – could any of these be adapted for their entertainment value for older people? Country or county publications might also be an ideal target market, especially if the games (or memories) have a regional flavour, and aimed at local fetes, fund-raising and church bazaars. Try introducing 'how to play ... to the How-To websites. And don't forget that there's quite a lucrative market place for writing games and puzzles – and telling people how to complete them. Look at how many games and puzzle books you can find at your local newsagent if that's your interest.

Pastimes

Hobby and collectors' magazines may often take a bit of finding but every interest will have its own publication, members' newsletter or website. This category covers every kind of collecting from stamps to vintage aeroplanes; and hobbies from crochet to canal boating. In fact, *anything* anyone does to 'pass the time' could probably fit into this subject, and it doesn't have to be a weekly or monthly activity. My own list would be rather boring as my work (writing) is also my hobby but it does mean that I get to do a lot of reading for pleasure. I also have an impressive collection of classic Japanese samurai films and well remember the National Film Theatre's 1982 season, although I missed the 2002 NFT's season by the legendary Akira Kurosawa. A large number of people, however, collect very small items and it's always difficult knowing how to store or display them ...

How To Display Family Memorabilia

If we are followers of the *Antiques Roadshow*, we will know that memorabilia is becoming more and more popular. It may start with a few small family pieces and grow into a vast hoard, but more often than not it is restricted to a small collection of personal photographs, medals and personal items from a family member or friend. The problem is knowing *how* to display them, without creating another dust trap!

- A personalised deep-sided picture frame can be purpose-made by a local picture framer, who can set the selected items inside the sealed case.
- Glass-topped coffee table display cabinets can be lined with an appropriate fabric and kept locked, especially if any of the objects are valuable.
- Lit from above, small glass-fronted, former kitchen wall units can provide a perfect display area for larger objects. Replace wooden shelves with glass.
- Fit modern box-type display units with a sheet of Perspex or glass added to the front and painted to suit your room.
- Small, revolving shop counter display cases come in all shapes and sizes and can be utilised to hold memorabilia, small antiques, etc.

Conclusion

Any of these display ideas can be refurbished or designed to suit any décor, whether traditional or modern. Most can be picked up at second-hand emporiums, car boot sales or on eBay.

There must be hundreds of ideas for storing or displaying collections, or the photographs recording the results of our pastimes. And each pastime will offer the opportunity to provide handy How-To hints, together with photographs illustrating the articles – which is an additional selling point for an editor. Collecting is a popular theme so lots of opportunities for 'how to spot a bargain' for the car-boot aficionados.

Do you have any How-To advice to help solve problems relating to pastime activities? What are your own pastimes? How can your advice and experience benefit others? Have you become expert on any sort of collectables?

Marketplace

These will, of course, be specialist magazines and websites, and the exercises will require some extra research on the part of the writer to identify the level of expertise required to write for each individual publication. Hobbies and pastime magazines is one area where the beginner/amateur is encouraged to share their experiences with other enthusiasts. At one writers' workshop we had a lady who collected and made miniature dolls especially for doll's houses, and after a bit of encouragement was persuaded to submit an article to a doll's house magazine – the result was a regular column. There is a limited marketplace for full-length books but the opportunities are there if your pastime is related to subjects such as canal-boating, antique collecting, etc., which have a larger following.

Build Your Portfolio

Writing How-To's about games and pastimes will require a certain amount of attention to detail, since the readers may not be fully aware of the 'rules' of gamesmanship and collecting – and there is nothing more frustrating than missing information in what is supposed to be a step-by-step guide. If in doubt give the finished How-To to a friend who knows *nothing* about the subject, and ask them if the instructions are easy to follow. Remember to credit any sources you use for reference.

Games: Exercise 16

The interest in traditional games has gone into decline since the advent of computer technology. For example, it's more convenient to play computer chess than setting up a board with its individual carved pieces for each game. Talk to older members of the family or community about how they amused themselves as children – can any of this information be adapted for today's participation (see **Entertainment**), entertaining children during the school holidays, and fund-raising activities?

Pastimes: Exercise 17

Hobbies and pastimes are usually written from an enthusiast's perspective and useful How-To's will come from those who have discovered how to solve problems and difficulties. Go on to the Internet and find out how many sites are dedicated to your particular interest, as there may be opportunities to add a How-To piece to their newsletter, blog or Facebook. This is also another area where we can pick the brains of family and friends if they indulge in interesting pastimes – but again, get them to check you submission before sending it off in case of errors.

The Half-way Mark:
Time for a Progress Report

In reality, you will probably have *not* written a single How-To article by this stage – because like all normal people you will be reading the book through from beginning to end, to see if there are any useful ideas you can utilise to spark off your own How-To writing. After all, that's why you bought the book in the first place. All How-To books are written as a step-by-step guide but we need to read them through once to get the 'feel' for the author's technique: the procedure we all use to accomplish getting our point across to the reader. This technique is another thing you'll need to understand and develop within your own writing because each writer's approach *is* different; reflecting our personality, and holding the reader's attention as we share experiences.

My own personal technique is to settle down for a cosy chat and this is the same whether it be tutoring workshops or online novel writing; editing *The New Writer*; features for magazines or writing my MB&S books. I try to make it sound easy ... friendly ... accessible ... with the use of family reminiscences, personal anecdote, observation, colloquialism, one-liners, and, what I am told, my own 'inimitable turn of phrase'. I talk about 'us' and 'we' as though we are all starting off on this journey together, despite the fact that I now have over 30 book titles to my credit. Not to mention over 20 years' experience as editor of a creative writing magazine.

A writer's technique *is* important because this is what makes a reader *want* to read on and absorb the information on offer. At this stage you may be a beginner starting out on the great Himalayan trek towards publication; or a more experienced writer attempting a new writing discipline – hopefully you will be thinking *both*:

This isn't as hard as it looks
AND
This is much more difficult than it looks

The first thought will arise because you've been playing little mind games with yourself as you read, to try and come up with something even more interesting and obscure in order to out-think the author in each category. While the second will be a result of realising that simple How-To articles actually take a lot of *thought* before coming up with something that has genuine editor appeal, and realising that it requires more than just a recorded series of facts. **This is the first step in convincing ourselves that there is a niche for us in this rapidly expanding genre.** As easy as How-To writing can be, there are a lot of writers who have difficulty in thinking outside the box when it comes to generating fresh ideas and hopefully this book will help you to understand what is probably the largest marketplace in the English-speaking world – and the world is waiting to read what *you* have to say.

As a good starting point, we can take a leaf out of *Writing From Life: How to turn your personal experience into profitable prose* (How-To Books), where Lynne Hackles observes that everyone has certain skills and urges writers to write down all the things we can do, or used to do. "This could prove a time-consuming exercise so list only what comes to mind now. You can add to your list as you read through this chapter." Or in our case - *chapters.* Your list should also include interests and hobbies past and present, including things you've collected; all the jobs you've had since leaving school; and places you've visited – write them down now in your How-To notebook for future reference.

One of the UK's most popular How-To authors, Lynne Hackles, has books with How-To Books, Aber Publishing and Compass Books because the publishers recognise that she is a past master at writing within the genre. Whether she's telling us how to go about *Writing From Life* (How-To Books), *Ghostwriting* (Aber), or imparting *Handy Hints For Writers* (Compass) we follow her instructions with a smile, and since her motto is 'never let the truth get in the way of entertainment', we are certain that her self-deprecatory tutoring technique will not be a disappointment! "Everyone," she says, "has a subject they can, or do, specialise in. Maybe you thought you didn't, but you'd be wrong. You may have several. Your specialist subject may be sitting in your Personal Experience file. If it's not already there then it will be by the end of this chapter."

Taking all this encouragement on board, *this* is our starting point for examining the skills *we* have, and learning how to turn them into an article someone will want to read in order to find out How-To do something. As we've seen from the first 17 exercises in this book, it *is* possible to have some sort of advice to offer on just about any topic, providing we fully understand the 'viewpoint' we need to be taking. If we're beginners or outsiders ourselves, then we need to write for beginners and outsiders. As we discussed under **Business & Corporate**, for example, it may be necessary to take the role of the customer/consumer; while with **Computers & Electronics**, as we observed earlier, the 'know-nots' may have a greater advantage over the 'know-alls', because we usually have a vast storehouse of difficulties that 'techies' would never dream of viewing as a problem.

In **Arts & Entertainment** we raised the point that enthusiastic amateurs are often better at recognising the need for basic How-To advice because they are still at the stage where there are silly, niggling little things that require explanation, and which many people would be too embarrassed to ask about for fear of ridicule in more exalted company. **Culture & Society** made us aware that every one of us is unique, and that no one can have access to the same experiences – which means we, as individuals, have the ability to generate unique responses to situations – and be in a position to offer How-To advice to others. And **Education** affects everyone – from pre-school to obtaining a university degree, pupils, parents, grandparents and family friends all become embroiled in the lengthy and expensive process.

Fashion & Style reminds us that How-To fashion and style tips need to be aimed at the specific age group reading each target magazine or newspaper. As far as **Food & Drink** are concerned, the world's media is obsessed with the subject and from anorexia to obesity, the genre caters for every palette, food fad and household budget.

And the larger your family and circle of friends, the easier it will be to draw on material suitable for How-To hints and articles for the **Friends & Family** category.

Games & Pastimes, of course, can be aimed at adults as well as children – and there are hundreds of traditional games that can be updated to bring fun to any form of organised entertainment and fund-raising events.

At this stage we should also realise that the term 'How-To' is a collective expression for *any* piece of writing that is instructional in content. According to Wikipedia, it is

> an informal, often short, description of how to accomplish some specific task … usually overly simplified to help non-experts … can range from brief directions to aid in performing a task one is unfamiliar with, to full-length books, generally intended to assist or inspire life-changing methods and attitudes. They occur in the 'self-help' genre, business books, and the hobby industry.

Just for the record, one of the earliest How-To books was published in 1569 by Thomas Wight and entitled, *A booke of the arte and maner, how to plant and graffe all sortes of trees: With divers other new practise, by one of the Abbey of Saint Vincent in Fraunce* by Leonard Mascall. And perhaps the most famous full-length book of all time in the genre is *How to Win Friends and*

Influence People, written by Dale Carnegie in 1936.

This means, of course, that the term 'How-To' does not have to appear in the title of our work, but it does immediately sum up exactly what our writing is about. If our title is obscure, with no How-To sub-heading to give any indication of the content, then a publisher or editor may overlook our submission – and a reader seeking advice on a given subject may over look your title on Amazon.

If you feel the urge to stop reading and start writing, this halfway mark provides a natural break in which you can get onto the computer and start composing your first How-To article – and thinking about where you are going to send it. Go back over the first 17 lessons and make a note of those you think look the most promising – and which look the most difficult.

It's also possible that you're already mentally formulating the idea of a full-length book and as we're only at the list-making stage of learning 'how to write How-To's', begin by making a list in your notebook of ten appropriate chapter headings as shown in the example in Chapter 1. As you think of the additional information that needs to be included in each chapter, add to the list until you have a further ten sub-headings. As explained earlier, you'll know if you have enough material for a full-length book if you can comfortably write 45,000 words, broken down into approximately ten separate chapters; divided by ten sub-headings for each chapter. This means each chapter will contain around 4,500 words; and each sub-heading approximately 450 words – the equivalent of ten mini articles. But first we need to find out if there is a demand for our work.

The best way to check on the range of How-To topics available in our specific subject area is to go onto the Internet and type 'How To ...' into the browser and go through the results. If we type in 'How to write ...' for example, the choices that come up include ... how to write a cover letter, a c.v., a book, a song .... If we add the word 'play' then the results come up ... how to write a play, a play review, a play format, a play for kids ... When we select the full subject heading to browse we then get a listing of all the related websites, blogs, Facebooks, etc., that come under that category. To find out how many How-To books there are currently available on your proposed subject, go to www.amazon.com 'Books' and you will find a list of competing titles and authors.

Or go onto the specific How-To websites such as www.makeuseof.com and see which topics have already been covered online. To give an example of the vastness of the online How-To market, Wikipedia cites the following:

wikiHow is a web-based and wiki-based community, consisting of an extensive database of How-To guides. wikiHow's mission is to build the world's largest and highest quality How-To manual. The site started as an extension of the already existing eHow website, and has evolved to host over 143,000 How-To articles. In January 2012, wikiHow had 35.5 million unique readers from over 200 countries or territories. These 35.5 million different people visited it a total of over 44 million times in the month.

As MakeUseOf rightly points out, How-To's are excellent problem solvers, providing

quick, easy-to-follow and non-overwhelming solutions to one or another problem that pop-up during daily routines. People love them, especially when they're free, regardless whether it's a step-by-step guide ... the amount of freely available, user-contributed How-To's out there is staggering. There is something for everyone: ranging from fun stuff i.e. how to make an invisible bookshelf, imitate gunshot wounds and even open up a Coke machine, to more practical stuff i.e. how to negotiate a raise or tie a tie. All categorized, commented and rated by users like you and me.

The Internet provides us with more information than we could ever hope to use in a lifetime, but this does have its drawbacks. No matter what the subject, your browser will always come up with the most popular and/or frequently used websites – **and so will everyone else's search.** A University recently complained that students were using the most popular material verbatim from the Internet for their theses, with some not even bothering to remove the website's headers from the print out! This meant, of course, that hundreds of students were using the same text to produce a dissertation that should have been based on *original* research. By learning to think outside the box, we should also be looking for *original* material, so don't rely solely on the Internet for your research – link into Wikipedia for checking dates and spellings by all means, but don't copy the text unless you acknowledge the source!

Research on the Internet is quick and easy but it's also addictive, so beware of wasting time. And at this stage of learning *How To Write For The How-To Market*, we need to remain focussed and return to our study. We've made our list of skills, interests, hobbies, work experience and places we've been. We have a list of ideas that look the most promising; we've completed some hands-on market research with the How-To sites on the Internet; and we've been getting a good idea of what writing for the How-To market involves. **We have subtly moved from being an observer to being a participant, even if we've yet to draft our first How-To piece.**

Chapter Eleven

Health & Beauty

Health and beauty topics must be about level pegging with food and drink when it comes to the number of magazine articles and books currently in publication. More and more people are choosing to take greater responsibility for their own health and beauty regimes because we recognise that we can influence our health and appearance by making improvements to our lifestyle – better diets, more exercise and less stress. There's quite a large target market here once we've learned to think outside the box, from simple health hints and beauty tips to full-length books.

Health

Look for something different – health care is becoming more topical, so it *is* necessary to avoid the obvious when writing about health issues, which often require a more in-depth approach than mere beauty tips. Cosmetic surgery and dentistry would come under this heading, as would all other minor corrective surgery from bunions and in-growing toenails to laser eye treatment. We can even broaden our scope for writing about historical health issues, and two useful titles that sit on my bookshelf are *An Ancient Egyptian Herbal* by Lise Manniche and *Ancient Egyptian Medicine* by John F Nunn – both by British Museum Press.

The idea for finding out more about the health hazard of radon gas came from a leaflet that was dropped through the door, and because when selling my last property the buyer requested a radon gas test before going ahead with the purchase.

How To Check for Radon Gas in Your Home

The level of radon gas in the area is another question that often arises when buying or selling a house, and in some cases, a high level of radon can affect the sale of a property. Purchasers are sometimes advised to delay or decline a purchase if the seller has not successfully abated radon to an acceptable level. But what is radon gas...

- Radon is a naturally occurring radioactive gas formed in the earth by the decay of uranium, which is present in small quantities in all rocks and soil. It cannot be seen, smelt or tasted and can only be detected with special equipment.
- For a long while radon has been associated with lung cancer and is believed to be in particles in the air that, when inhaled, are deposited in the airways and on lung tissue to give a radiation dose that can cause lung cancer. Smokers and former smokers are at the greatest risk.
- Radon gas moves through the soil and can enter buildings through cracks in the floors, gaps around pipes and cables. Radon that surfaces outdoors quickly dilutes to harmless levels.
- Minor amounts of radon may also come from building materials and from domestic water supplies.
- Indoor radon concentrations can vary considerably from day to day due to changes in the weather, ventilation, etc. Keep your house well ventilated both upstairs and down.
- There is an interactive online map that tells postcode residents and business people if their premises are at risk of exposure to radon gas.
- Beware of the junk mail coming through your door offering to measure the amount of radon gas in your home, and to provide a 'radon remediation service'. These can be costly and there's no guarantee that the service is genuine.

Conclusion

There are relatively simple tests for radon gas, but these tests are not commonly done, even in areas of known systematic hazards. Radon test kits are commercially available. The short-term radon test kits used for screening purposes are inexpensive, in many cases free. The kit includes a collector that the user hangs in the lowest liveable floor of the house for two to seven days. The user then sends the collector to a laboratory for analysis. Long term kits, taking collections for up to one year, are also available. An open-land test kit can test radon emissions from the land before construction begins. To find out more about radon gas go to Wikipedia.

...Magazine editors are always looking for clear, comprehensive, straightforward andencouraging How-To information and advice about methods of improving health and beauty techniques. We are also becoming increasingly aware that there are other natural methods – some new, some very ancient – that can help use to look and feel good on a daily basis. Health hazards are always of interest to editors and publishers if we go for an original approach, such as Dave Reavely's *Healthy Eating and Pollution Protection for Kids;* Austen Hayes's *The Good Heart* or Marie-Clare Wilson's *Seasonal Awareness and Wellbeing.* There could also be opportunities for full-length LifeStyle proposals here such as Sarah-Beth Watkins' *The Lifestyle Writer* - and how-to cope with serious illness from the viewpoint of the sufferer or a close family member that would help others in the same predicament.

Health scares are always alarming and most of us suffer from them at some stage in our lives. How did you cope? What methods/treatment did you take to overcome them? Have you any useful information to share, such as the right organisations to contact for help?

Marketplace

It often appears that people are becoming obsessive about health and for this reason there is a very wide market place for 'how to cope' with various health problems, both personal and family issues. According to *Eating For Good Health*, our health and general well-being can be determined by what we eat and even minor changes to a diet can help strengthen the resistance to many illnesses from the common cold to heart disease, cancer, hypertension and stroke. Start by examining the various women's magazines, including health and beauty publications, and health care journals. Remember that you *don't* have to be a professional to write about a health problem that causes wide-ranging difficulties within the family, and writing about how to cope, or contact the relevant health departments can be of immeasurable help to others in the same position. Aromatherapy and domestic plant medicine could also be aimed at the MB&S outlets; and don't forget the wide range of parenting magazines. Writing for the disability markets also offers a lot of opportunities, providing we observe certain rules in the use of emphasis and language; the readership want to know about lifestyle improvements, new resources and technologies in the home and workplace, sporting activities, etc.

This is also a perfect market for the full-length How-To book such as Deborah Bates' *Your Personal Tuning Fork: The Endocrine System*, Lovera and David Miller's *Womanopause: Stop Pausing and Start Living*, Nancy Gordon's *Guiding Philosophy for the Future of Health Care*, or David Gerow Irving's *The Protein Myth*.

Beauty

Some of the earliest medical preparations were ointments, lotions and balms for the care of skin and hair – and these topics are still the most popular for the beauty pages of women's magazines. Simple preparations such as - extracting the juice from a cabbage in a blender for use as a lotion for acne; or adding 4 tablespoons of dried violets to 1 litre of cold water (cover, heat slowly to boiling point; cool for 15 minutes and strain) applied as a compress for inflamed skin - are always of interest. On the other hand we have historical references to draw on, such as Lise Manniche's *Sacred Luxuries: Fragrance, Aromatherapy and Cosmetics in Ancient Egypt* to liven up our writing. Study as many publications as you can, and find the formula that suits your level of writing skill – for example:

How To Treat Dandruff Naturally

There are numerous natural preparations to improve the condition of your hair and scalp – and dandruff in particular may respond to a herbal treatment. Dandruff is a common condition: dead skin that leaves white flakes in the hair and on clothes. The usual cause of mild dandruff is a dry scalp.

- Rosemary is a herb widely used for toning the scalp – it has astringent properties and make hair shine. Use a standard infusion of rosemary as a hair rinse (followed by rinsing with water), or soak 280g of fresh rosemary in 600 ml of ordinary shampoo and use for 2 weeks.
- As an alternate to rosemary, a lemon juice rinse can help if dandruff sticks to the hair and scalp. Add 2 tablespoons to 600 ml water).
- Drinking an infusion of red clover and nettle may help clear dandruff by improving overall skin health.
- Taking evening primrose oil capsules may reduce over dryness of the skin, including the scalp.

Conclusion

The build-up of dandruff may be due to infrequent brushing, poor blood circulation, overuse of commercial hair products, or an unhealthy diet. Natural shampoos can help tone the scalp and get rid of dandruff, but if the condition persists consult your doctor.

Some problems, such as bad skin, poor conditioned hair, or broken and split nails may be prevented by healthy eating but unlike hints and tips, this beauty How-To would require a full-length article to provide an in-depth step by step guide. A much simple approach would be 'how to cure bitten fingernails' or 'how to choose the best nail polish remover'. Beauty tips are generally aimed at improving the general appearance of the reader but some editors might appreciate the 'then and now' slant using material from old recipe books. When I worked for the cosmetic company back in the 1970s, it had a policy of not testing the products on animals, and staff members were asked to volunteer instead – we had free cosmetics in exchange for conducting skin tests for new preparations. Not many people know that …

Beauty hints such as adding 6 drops of lavender essential oil to 1 pint of distilled water to make a natural deodorant, needs little How-To advice and can provide valuable 'fillers'.

Marketplace

Study the health, women's and MB&S magazines to see what kind of material the editor is accepting on beauty topics. Unless written by a skin-care professional, the majority of articles in this category are simplistic How-To's on keeping skin and hair healthy, and the old fashioned remedies are often just as effective as modern beauty products. There are also plenty of opportunities for full-length How-To's with a difference, such as Caroline T Ward's *Four Faces of Woman*.

Build Your Portfolio

Everyone has their own favourite How-To beauty tips and hints for staying healthy, and this is a perfect opportunity to exploit what may merely be part of our own daily or weekly routine. Some of the simplest may also be some of the best, such as using cold teabags or cucumber for the relief of tired eyes. Research our subject well and we can find all sorts of little snippets to add interest to our writing.

Health: Exercise 18

Keep this How-To simple and gossipy – and submit as a 'Letter to the Editor', particularly if the subject has been featured in a previous issue. This shows that we have bothered to familiarise ourselves with the publication and although payment is modest, there are often expensive prizes given for the 'Star Letter'. Recipes for healthy eating – especially for children - could also be included (see **Food**) in this section – for example one 6 fl oz glass of fresh fruit juice meets our daily need of vitamin C.

Beauty: Exercise 19

The same rules apply for this category – but with even more opportunities. As well as women's and MB&S publications, there are numerous regional magazine outlets for How-To topics linked to localised producers of natural beauty products. Beauty, of course is in the eye of the beholder, so the odd historical piece could reveal how ladies of the past diced with death in using preparations of arsenic (to make the skin appear a bluish white) and atropine (for dilating the pupils) to enhance their appearance.

Chapter Twelve

Home & Garden

Another topic that occupies a lot of space in colour supplements and magazines, as well as advertorials in local 'free papers', is anything to do with home improvements, make-overs, and gardening. Like gardening, home improvements can also be a seasonal affair, so plan ahead. In both categories, we can also stretch our imaginations from 'how to do a garden make-over' to 'how to improve your lifestyle'.

Even simple hints such as 'how to clean paintbrushes' or maintain terracotta flowerpots comes under this heading. In fact, we can make it as easy or as extensive as we feel we can write about.

Home

Home, they say, is where the heart is and throughout our lives our taste and style changes – often dramatically. It's rare, however, that we discard *everything* from our past and often we need to rearrange our refurbishment around what we've already got in our possession. Or we may find some treasure at a car-boot or yard sale and need some How-To advice on how best to integrate it successfully into our home.

How To Start Collecting Antiques

Most of us start collecting antiques because we have been given something 'old' by a relative, or by a family friend. Or we may just see a fascinating piece that we just *have* to buy. Others find an antique discarded in a skip ... and so the interest begins. Today's collectors buy one piece at a time and often re-sell at a later date at auction, in order to buy something more expensive.

You will need:

An appropriate *Miller's Antiques Guide*

- We must also begin by realising that we don't have to have a complete home make-over before our collecting begins. An antique bronze, Clarice Cliff vase, or selection of Georgian snuff-boxes can look just as impressive against a contemporary décor.

- Before buying anything, it is necessary to decide on a 'purchase plan' and make sure that whatever you want to collect is within your price range. And that it is an investment rather than an indulgence.

- At the moment twentieth century is very much in vogue and Victorian isn't, which means if you happen to like Victoriana then you could pick up a bargain that will increase in value somewhere along the road, if not in the immediate future.

- Fifties, Sixties and Seventies is now very collectable and often appeals to the younger collector who may not be able to afford Art Deco.

- Decide on how you are going to display your collection to avoid clutter that collects dust and can be easily broken. China looks good on a cream-painted dresser, while glass sparkles behind glass and under lights; curios can be grouped in special picture-frame display boxes to enhance their interest.

- Keep your eye open for a limited number of 'star pieces' that will provide focal points in your home. They don't have to cost a fortune but they must be items that you love, and which will appreciate in value.

- Bearing these tips in mind, do your homework and read books on your chosen subject. Pay a visit to the antiques fairs, auctions, and the various 'antiques emporiums' dotted around the country. But don't be too eager to buy just yet – get a feel for the prices different dealers are asking.

- Judith Miller (of *Antiques Guide* fame) warns that some dealers don't put a price tag on their wares, they use a numbered code instead. When asked the price they consult the code book to see what they paid for it (which the buyer can't see) and then give a price depending on how affluent or keen you appear to be.

- When visiting an antiques fair, turn left once you've passed through the entrance. Most people will turn instinctively to the right, which means you can get to the bargains before the throng. If you've been unsuccessful in beating a dealer down early in the day, go back at the end of the fair, as they may be more inclined to take your offer rather than pack the piece up and take it home.

- If you are trying to match antiques such as chairs, always take a photograph of the pieces already in your possession for comparison.

Conclusion

By rule of thumb, any antiques we buy should not lose value the moment we take them home, but should steadily increase in value. Go for quality and avoid damaged goods. Don't fall for the dealer's hype – there are just as many dodgy dealers as there are good ones. Events organised by BADA and LAPADA guarantee that the antiques on sale are what their sales ticket says they are. If they're not, you've got comeback.

Home and lifestyle go together, so lots of How-To ideas about family issues also come under this umbrella, such as 'how to store sports equipment', general storage solutions, down-sizing everything - from moving house to CD collections. Or 'how to clean things – like marble fireplaces, old linen, books or silver plate. We all have a periodic 'spring clean' so what solutions have you found for those tiresome once-a-year jobs? And not forgetting the old chestnuts of removing dog and cat hair, red wine and Bolognaise sauce stains. There's always the problem of how and where to fit in a home office ... or dog bed; and *how* do you get those awful non-slip tiles to look clean!

Lots of scope for home-help How-To's – what family secrets can you divulge? How did you get the kids to throw away all those unwanted bits and pieces? Do you know of any charities/organisations that will take specific items such as old mobile phones, etc?

Marketplace

Virtually any magazine or newspaper will accept How-To tips on homes, especially if it is linked to advertising, so check with your local free newspaper to see if they will accept a short How-To piece to link with a forthcoming specialised home improvement feature. Women's weekly publications are the best bet for handy hints and Letters. If, on the other hand, you've had experience renovating an old property, then you should be able to find other How-To opportunities in the various building trade journals. Do bear in mind, however, that the glossy monthlies usually require lots of professional standard photographs to support a submission. If we're looking at furnishing or decorating a room for a child, we can look at something for parenting magazines. And, since every little helps, there are in-store supermarket magazines that encourage readers to share their ideas – especially if using 'own brand' products.

Finally, try pushing the concept of 'home' to its limit as in the case of Lindsay Holton's *The Secret of Home* or Marian Van Eke McCain's *Downshifting Made Easy*.

Garden

Outdoor living comes under the heading of gardening and offers even more opportunities for How-To lifestyle improvements as well as traditional gardening tips for allotments, patios, water features, etc. 'How to attract wildlife to the garden' is high on everyone's agenda these days and this may provide quite a few opportunities if you encourage children to participate. And on the down-side *how* do you control slugs? I must confess to finding those beer-soaked bodies distasteful, and rather reminiscent of Clarence and the vat of Malmesbury! Nevertheless, nearly everyone is a gardening fanatic these days even if they are restricted to a few pots on a balcony – so masses of opportunity for mini How-To's such as:

How To 'Age' Garden Ornaments

If you want to get rid of that 'straight from the garden centre' look about your pots, tubs, containers and statuary, there is a simple way to age them – naturally!

What you'll need:

3 inch paintbrush
Pot of natural yoghurt
Soot from the chimney (optional)

- Mix the soot and yoghurt at the rate of one tablespoon of soot to one small pot of yogurt. This should be sufficient for one good-sized container.
- Paint the mixture onto the container and leave to dry. If it rains before the mixture is dry, the yoghurt will wash off and the process will need repeating.
- If the container or statue is made from reconstituted stone and is rough textured, work the bristles of the brush into all the cracks and crevices.

Conclusion

This treatment will darken the 'stone' instantly, as well as encouraging moss and lichen to grow. Using plain yoghurt will not darken the stone, but it will cause it to change colour. The treatment will not work on plastics tubs and containers.

If it's linked to growing things, like 'how to grow herbs on the kitchen window sill', there will be an editor who likes the way you've put a new slant on a popular topic. Or how to stop brown patches on the lawn (see **Animals**) if you have a female dog, is something that would even interest non-gardeners. Wild-life gardening hints and tips are also popular, especially what *not* to feed them.

Have you any simple gardening How-To hints to share – even if it's only growing seedlings in cardboard egg boxes?

Marketplace

Some element of gardening appears in just about every weekly magazine and newspaper, so begin by studying the gardening supplements in the weekend newspapers and see how they present everything from mini How-To's to full length instructional articles. Don't forget that garden furniture, lighting and barbeque equipment also comes under the heading of 'gardening' – as do swimming pools, fishponds and water features. Extend your research to include the numerous gardening magazines that could also be interested in How-To pieces on keeping chickens, attracting wildlife and pet-proof gardens (see **Animals**). Don't forget that creative writing magazines will welcome articles on ' how to write for' with a specific target market in mind.

Build Your Portfolio

This is another area where simple is best to start a writing career – feature articles are usually written by professionals and/or celebrities but 'fillers' will offer plenty of opportunities for beginners. Look around your own home and try to create a How-To piece relating to each room in the house – cleaning techniques are always useful and old-fashioned methods are always interesting. Then move to the garden shed and see how many ideas that brings to mind ...

Home: Exercise 20

Storage and money-saving How-To's would probably be the writer's best bet for this category if you can come up with some original ideas. What about small utensils that are invaluable in a well-run kitchen – or do you use them for a different purpose for which they were intended? Have you inherited some implement from your mother or grandmother you still use, like my pre-war mint chopper?

Garden: Exercise 21

Most specialist gardening publications positively encourage beginners to submit their ideas, Letters and How-To's, and even simple but original ideas such as 'how to care for ...' or store gardening tools and equipment would certainly catch the editor's eye. What about cleaning paths, patios, driveways, etc., - do you have an effective method that would provide a simple How-To guide? Or keeping the neighbour's cat off the asparagus bed - and the squirrels off the bird feeders.

Chapter Thirteen

Legal

Basically anything that involves a bit of paper requiring a witnessed signature comes under the heading of 'legal' – which is not necessarily binding. If you have legal training then the professional journals and monthly glossies can offer a wider marketplace, but for the rest of us, there are still topics to be written about. Everyone, at some stage in their life is involved in legal wrangling in some form or another – marriage, divorce, custody, buying or renting a house, taking out a loan, signing an insurance agreement, changing a name …

How To Change Your Name by Deed Poll

People decide to change their name for a variety of reasons and your age, nationality and country of residence are the factors that determine whether you can apply for a Deed Poll to change your name within the UK. There are just two simple steps:

What you'll need:

An Official Deed Poll Form

- You first need to acquire your Deed Poll documentation, either online or from the Solicitor's Law Stationary Society. There is no need to pay to change your name legally in the UK. All you need is a 'deed of change'.
- When you have your Deed Poll document, you simply sign and date it in the presence of an independent witness such as a friend, neighbour or work colleague.
- A change of name Deed Poll must contain three declarations and by signing, dating and having your signature witnessed you are declaring that the use of your previous

name has been abandoned; your new name will be used at all times; all persons are required to address you by your new name only.

• Give some thought to the name you intend using for the rest of your life: this needs to be something that fits comfortably with your personality and not cause embarrassment in the years to come.

Conclusion

Your signed Deed Poll is documentary proof of your change of name, which you then need to show to all government departments, companies and organisations that hold your personal records, instructing them to change your name. You can also apply for a new British passport, driving licence, chequebook, credit cards etc. to be reissued in your new name.

Legal stuff of interest to writers also includes subjects such as copyright, libel and contracts, which, sooner or later will apply to anyone with a serious interest in producing the written word. There are also the quirks and foibles of local by-laws that can provide endless hours of amusement and profitable How-To's for a wide variety of magazines. Motor tax (see **Motoring**) and television licences (see **Home**) are also legal requirements, so how to apply for either of these could provide another How-To idea for those taking them out for the first time. If you or your family have been involved in any neighbour disputes, this 'how to deal with the issue' could be of interest to the women's or lifestyle magazines. For example there was a recent falling out over the noise of a neighbour's *wind-chimes* – and the local council ruled they represented noise pollution!

Have you experienced or come into contact with any legal issues that could be turned into a simple How-To for the benefit of others?

Marketplace

Some market research is needed for this category because, without legal qualifications, it needs a personal experience twist to make it acceptable for an editor. Nevertheless, there are numerous topics that can interest a wide readership, such as 'how to consider making a prenuptial/cohabitation agreement', which I had accepted by an online How-To editor – although I listed it under **Weddings**! But that's the way *my* mind works. Study the weekly women's magazines if you feel you can produce a concise legal How-To; while more homely legal issues, such as home insurance and noise pollution, might suit a student magazine.

Build Your Portfolio

A slightly more difficult exercise but it is possible to marry up a marketable How-To on a legal issue with the right editor, if you put your mind to it and think outside the box. Have any friends or family experienced minor legal problems that were quickly solved, or could have been easily prevented, with the right kind of advice?

Legal: Exercise 22

Don't be tempted to tackle bigger issues in a brief How-To article as it will only emphasise your status as a beginner writer. Think closer to home on the subject of tenancy agreements, mobile phone contracts or personal loans – these are the common, everyday occurrences that can be horribly confusing when undertaking them for the first time, especially if they go wrong.

Chapter Fourteen

Motoring

The subject of motoring isn't restricted to cars and if we take a while to study the amount of magazines devoted to the topic we find a multitude of How-To topics that don't actually require an intimate working knowledge of the mechanics of a vehicle. Simple things such as 'how to pass a driving test', applying for a provisional driving licence, and 'how to tax a motor vehicle' will all apply to someone doing it for the first time. Then there are the various adaptations required for children, dogs, the elderly or disabled in order to make motoring easier. Thinking outside the box, the following article was produced following the decision that a motor home was the ideal solution for holidays that would allow us to take the dogs with us.

How To Choose the Right Motor Home

More and more people are buying motor homes as a means of holidaying because it gives more freedom in moving from place to place, and provides a much more comfortable means of travel than towing the traditional caravan. Before you begin, make sure you set yourself a firm budget – and stick to it. If you are not familiar with motorhomes, study the classified pages in the specialist magazine before you view any vehicles. 'Practical Motorhome' magazine advises that we should see as many different motorhomes as we can before making a decision.

You'll soon start to get a feel for what represents good value for money. Try to build a relationship with a local dealership, or at least one that's not too far from home. That way, if problems arise or if you need some general maintenance work carried out, the cost of return visits to their premises shouldn't be too hard on your wallet.

What you will need:

A selection of motorhomes magazines.

- Buying from a dealer may be more expensive than buying privately, but a dealer has a duty to tell you of any problems and the cost of rectifying them, as well as giving the van a pre-delivery inspection before you collect it. You'll also be offered at least a few months' warranty on used models, which is something that you're unlikely to get from a private vendor.
- Also be aware of what weight of vehicle you can legally drive; the amount of home parking space available; and what size you feel comfortable driving.
- If your children have left home, or you plan to have a child, how much room will you need to cope with babies and visitors - for a day, or a week? If you're planning your retirement and intend to take longer trips, or visit friends around the UK, will there be enough room to have a bit of personal space? Don't compromise too much on space – for two people go for a 4-berth.
- Do you require extra headroom for you to be able to stand up straight, or manoeuvre easily? Make sure two people can pass each other when one is working in the kitchen, and get to the lavatory when other occupants are asleep.
- Colour schemes are a matter of personal taste, but 'Practical Mororhome' points out how different styles favour certain seasons: dark woods can be a bit oppressive in summer, and bright colour schemes can appear cold in winter. Try to assess how much daylight the windows and rooflight will provide on dull or rainy days.
- Fixed beds are the most comfortable, but they have their limitations. Corner beds have cut-off corners, reducing one

partner's legroom. Overcab and garage beds will have restricted headroom and one person will have to climb over the other if they want to go to the bathroom during the night. Check the quality and condition of the mattresses.

- How much storage space, equipment and worksurface area do you require. Do you require an oven or microwave, fridge/freezer, washing machine. If you're unsure about how much space you will need, consider what you would need for a week's touring.
- Do you need plenty of space to relax? Could one of the beds be used as a sofa? Could the swivel seats become recliners?
- How many people can sit at the table and eat comfortably? Check for table extensions and adjustment mechanisms, and how easy is it to serve food to the table from the kitchen?
- If you plan to stay on sites all the time, the lavatory or shower space is not a major consideration. Many washrooms are narrow, so the simplest way to test whether there's enough room for your needs is to physically act out showering and washing.

Conclusion

A motorhome gives an ideal home from home, and the chance to travel around the country without sticking to a timetable. You can move on whenever you feel like it and, as an added incentive, it makes it easier to take the dog on holiday!

The more we delved into the subject, the more we realised how complex the decision would be to choose the right vehicle – and the selection of motor home magazines also revealed how detailed articles needed to be for an editor to accept them. Motoring How-To tips don't have to be as complex as this one, but there are a multitude of opportunities for more modest submissions such as 'how to cope with your dog on a car journey' or 'how to deal with children's rubbish on a long journey'.

Have you any personal motoring How-To's that would make travelling by car easier both at home and abroad? What about the pitfalls of buying certain types of vehicle? Or how to measure comfort in a car before buying.

Marketplace

There are literally hundreds of specialist magazines across the world that fall under the umbrella of 'motoring' including motorcycling, car mechanics, vintage cars, caravaning and motorhomes - before we go into the more elitist field of motor racing and classic cars. Then we have publications that include articles on family motoring and holidays (see **Travel**) that really open up the market place for How-To information and 'how to get the best deals out of your car insurance'. Daily, weekend and local newspapers (including the free papers) all feature something on motoring, and can offer both ideas and opportunities for freelance How-To pieces. Then there are the magazines for truckers – so how about some handy How-To's for making life more pleasant on the road?

Build Your Portfolio

Ladies, don't skip over this exercise thinking it only applies to the chaps – even if you only ride in a car for a weekly shop at Tesco's then you'll have some snippet of advice to impart about motoring and motorists – even if it's only for the Letters page.

Motoring: Exercise 23

If you've ever been on a long distance motoring trip, then you've got something to write about because some publications will also accept How-To touring tips; not to mention the disasters that happened along the way – especially those that could have been prevented with a little bit of How-To advice.

Chapter Fifteen

Personal Finance

In the present financial climate, this is a topic that affects us all and there are lots of hints and tips that the How-To writer can pick up and utilise. Start by studying the personal financial section of the broadsheet newspapers – such as 'Your Money' from the Saturday *Telegraph* - and pay particular attention to the advertisements. One weekend supplement could provide you with as many as 20 How-To ideas, with all the information you need from websites to free information packs to bulk out your writing. This one for example:

How To Get Help with Debt

If you find yourself in debt, free help and advice services are provided by the Citizen's Advice Bureau and organisations such as the Consumer Credit Counselling Service (recently renamed StepChange Debt Charity), who will spend time to familiarise themselves with the problem and advise on what to do to pay creditors; how to keep a roof over your head; and ensure continuing services such as gas and electricity. The advice and help given is tailored to the individual and continues until you are out of trouble.

- Prepare details of all your debts, together with bank statements and any letters demanding payment.
- Over the telephone, a helpline advisor will usually perform an immediate assessment of the situation ending in emergency help, self-help material, or the offer of a counselling appointment.
- The advisor will consider your whole situation before recommending the best solution for your debt problems.

StepChange for example, offers free advice and the assessment can be completed online in under 20 minutes, anonymously and with no commitment.

- The first priority, wherever possible, is to allow for essential expenditure, priority debts and living expenses. The advisor will assess whether the client has enough left over to make an offer of repayment to other creditors. If so, creditors are asked to freeze interest, stop penalties and charges, accept a longer repayment period and sometimes a reduced sum.
- Your monthly payment will be calculated on the difference between your total monthly income and your total monthly expenditure.
- Arranging an official debit management plan via an independent agency lets your creditors know that you are serious about clearing your debts in the shortest possible timescale.
- Organisations such as Step Change deal with making payment offers to your creditors and all you have to do is make one payment to them, and they distribute it to all your creditors.

Conclusion

Personal debt usually results from a change in financial circumstances, caused by reduced income or overuse of credit, although relationship problems and changes in employment status are also common causes. Because of this, personal financial difficulties affect people from all walks of life and those on high incomes as well as those on low ones. The important thing is to remember that you are not alone, and that thousands of people have already been helped by debt management plans. Some debt management companies charge a fee for acting on your behalf – make sure you obtain a free service, so that all of your payment goes towards clearing your debts.

We all have to deal with personal finances when it comes to banking – the personal high street version, telephone, or online – and we've probably become quite expert on avoiding bank charges and overdrafts. The same applies to our private health care, various insurance policies, credit cards and direct debits. Also take into account that planning for our retirement used to focus on saving enough money to provide a decent income for when we stopped working – this is no longer the case. For instance: the income from a £100,000 pension pot 20 years ago was £15,640; today the income from the same amount is now down to £5,140! Everyone now has a vested interest in financial matters and simple home economies can save a considerable amount of money in a year. What are your methods for saving money on personal finances? Have you any How-To advice you can share? How do you build up your savings?

Marketplace

Again we are looking at a very wide range of publications that might take your How-To hints on saving money or personal finances because this subject is all about making our money last to the next payday. The popular television series *Super Scrimpers* can offer some very surprising savings when it comes to 'home economics' and this is the How-To advice that will find favour with editors. Look at the weekly women's and retirement magazines for both ideas and publishing opportunities, especially any cautionary tales about pensions. Online How-To sites are worth a look since this is a very popular area and you might come up with something slightly different. There are markets for full-length books on specific areas of personal investment and if you have the expertise then it could be worth investigating.

Build Your Portfolio

Most of the big supermarket chains have some form of

newsletter or promotional handouts and there may be opportunities for simple How-To hints relating to the store's own brand of merchandise (see **Home**). Explore this avenue ... as well as others. Use your own experiences of saving money to create interesting How-To's.

Exercise 24: Personal Finance

The online How-To sites are also interested in money-saving pieces and so are Letters to the Editor in the weekly women's magazines. How about 'how do you introduce children to the concept of regularly saving money?' – there must be as many ideas as there are grandmas. We sent the three youngest of my partner's grandchildren a £2 savings tin with £5 worth of coins inside, with the promise that the one who filled the tin first and banked the proceeds, would have their money doubled; the second would have half their total money doubled; and the third a quarter of their total doubled. Will it work? – the Post Office books are at the ready!

Chapter Sixteen

Pets & Animals

A popular topic that might not offer as many *paying* writing outlets as might be first imagined. Nevertheless there are all sorts of angles that can be explored, even if you're not a pet owner yourself. 'How to go on holiday with your pet' ... 'how to choose the right kennel/cattery' ... hotels and holiday cottages that cater for pet owners ... after all, *who* can you get to look after your pet boa constrictor while you're away? Remember: pets and animals don't always refer to dogs and cats ... nowadays folk keep all sorts of exotic pets, which provide plenty of opportunity for how to choose the right pet and not be swayed by kids' whims because they've seen something on telly! How-To pieces should put the responsibility for the well-being of the animal or bird fairly and squarely on the shoulders of would-be pet-owners whether adult or child.

Pets

Having a whole pack of greyhounds, you might think they *could* provide an endless supply of articles, but dog magazines appear only to be interested in rescue sob-stories as far as this breed is concerned. And although there are lots of opportunities for run-of-the-mill, how to care for various types of pet, again we must think outside the box for something different. The following was accepted by an onlineHow-To website, under a retirement category (See **Family**).

How To Provide for Your Pet if You Can't

We don't like to think that we may eventually be unable to care for our pets but sometimes it happens. We may die suddenly, become ill, or have to move into a care home. In cases like these, there are animal charities which can help with veterinary care, take your pet in and look after them for you, or find them a new home.

- Wood Green offers this re-homing service for free and provides an information pack that will give you all the information you need for making arrangements in your Will.
- Blue Cross will re-home pets and also provides veterinary care for pets whose owners cannot afford private vet's bills through their animal hospitals.
- Dogs Trust offers a free service in Canine Care Card that takes care of your dog if the worst should happen, and will find them a new home suited to their needs. It's easy to apply and once you are registered the Trust will send you a handy wallet-sized card to carry with you as you would a donor card.
- The Dogs Trust also operates the Hope Veterinary Entitlement Card (VEC) to help those dogs belonging to people who are homeless or in housing crisis and ensures that all dogs (whether they have a roof over their heads or not,) can receive free and subsidised professional veterinary care whenever they need it.

Conclusion

We never know what's around the corner, so make your arrangements now and keep your pet's details with your personal papers, Will, etc. If you are a vet or work with homeless people and would like more information on the VEC scheme call 020 7837 0006 or email hopeproject@dogstrust.org.uk

This article gave all the contact details for the different organisations, and also information about subsidised veterinary care for homeless people, which would make an interesting How-To piece for care professionals. Some people register their pets with the PAT (Pets As Therapy) scheme and how to qualify for this, would create another article. Since living in Ireland we've helped re-home over 80 retired greyhounds and still receive pictures from the very first one we sent out to Italy – reclining on his family's yacht cruising the Italian lakes! This prompted a 'how to adopt a retired greyhound' piece for publication.

Do you know someone who keeps unusual pets who could provide you with information or possibly an interview with lots of How-To advice included?

Marketplace

Pet How-To's have quite a wide appeal, especially when connected to voluntary schemes such as those mentioned above. Animal organisations such as the Blue Cross and Dog's Trust produce a regular newsletter for members and How-To pieces relating to pets adopted from these organisations would appeal to the editor. There are often problems arising with pets when family circumstances change such as moving house, a new baby or taking over a parent's pet for a short or long-term. Advice on how to cope with these situations could help others and might be appropriate for a wide range of magazines from mainstream to professional publications. Not to mention a full-length How-To book similar to Billy Roberts' *A Wag's As Good As A Smile* that looks at the healing power of pets.

Animals

Animals can provide a wealth of material, providing we avoid the mawkish sentimentality that often clouds this type of writing. The following How-To came from a friend who baby-sits local dogs in her own home when their owners go away; and people who keep all types of animals can be very useful when it comes to handy How-To hints and tips.

How To Remove the Smell of Fox Poo from the Dog

It doesn't matter how big the field, or how small the pile of fox poo – your dog will find it! Those dog owners who've tried to get rid of the smell will know that no matter how many shampooing sessions your pet is subjected to, nothing will shift it. Try this:

What you'll need:

Rubber gloves
Dog shampoo
Tomato ketchup

- Shampoo the area thoroughly with dog shampoo and rinse off with warm water.
- Apply a liberal amount of tomato ketchup to the area and work well into the fur.
- Rinse thoroughly with warm water and dry the dog. Do not re-shampoo.
- Remember to treat the collar with ketchup as the canvass or leather will also retain the smell.

Conclusion

This treatment works with both long and short-haired dogs, and prevents the need for the dog to spend the night in the shed! The same friend also recommended putting a tablespoon of tinned tomato on the bitch's dinner to prevent those horrible brown scald patches on the lawn. And with four girls and a half-acre lawn, we know it works!

Lots of people have a great fondness for animals without actually owning any, and animal How-To's could also cover 'how to arrange a surprise outing to a sanctuary or wild-life park'. There are also schemes to adopt both rescue and wild animals for a number of charities and how to do this for a birthday present could fit the bill. A small girl might love ponies and adopting one would provide her very own pony, together with a 'how to arrange a trip to Bransby Home For Horses' to meet the animal in its new home. Not to mention the prospect of 'how to volunteer to work for an animal charity'.

There are dozens of handy hints about pet-care or pet-related ideas that might be of interest or help to others. How many How-To's can you provide?

Marketplace

Aim your ideas at family orientated magazines and in particular, those catering for teenagers and younger children. Look at the websites for animal charities and see if they produce a newsletter. The Letters page in the pets' magazines might take How-To's similar to the example above, and if you have equine connections, study the marketplace and submit your handy hints to the one that is appropriate for the level of advice you're offering. And don't forget the farming, country and regional publications that could be interested in how to find rare breed owners and specialist welfare/rescue organisations in the area that encourage visitors. Books on caring for all sorts of pets have long been the staple diet of the How-To market but the keeping of animals is an emotive subject, so also think in terms of Mark Hawthorne's full-length book: *Striking At The Roots: A Practical Guide to Animal Activism.*

Build Your Portfolio

Most of the material you produce in this category will be non-paying, so keep it short and sweet – unless you can produce an interview-type of How-To with plenty of practical advice from a recognised expert in their field, then there should be a fee attached. Also think along the lines of what used to be called 'Nature Study' in schools and try pitching an article for younger children to encourage them to take an interest in discovering wild-life.

Pets: Exercise 25

Try offering to write How-To leaflets for your local pet shops, pet grooming parlours, kennels or riding stables - or suggest writing a series of pet themed 'advertorials' for the local free newspaper. It may attract a modest fee and provide you with repeat commissions. Short tips such as 'how to amuse a hamster' might fair better in the appropriate magazines, rather than a long, overly-sentimental piece about your pet.

Animals: Exercise 26

Items offering advice on how to attract wildlife into the garden will probably be more marketable than general animal pieces. Try the above exercise with pet shops selling wild bird food and local garden centres. Unless we have first-hand experience of a particular animal or bird it is doubtful whether we will be able to produce a saleable How-To, but we *can* offer How-To advice of where to see specific animals in the wild, rare breeds, etc., in terms of a **Travel** piece.

Chapter Seventeen

Sports & Fitness

This category can be written about by anyone that participates in any kind of sport or fitness programme, from beginner to Olympic athlete – even if it's only from the sidelines. Sport involves the whole family, whether they participate or not, so plenty of material here for 'how to cope with ...' and with the high-profile of the London 2012 Paralympics, it demonstrates that those with a disability need not be excluded from taking part in sporting events. The British Government has decided that there *is* a need to encourage competitive sport in the school curriculum and sports clubs all over the world will be expecting a surge of interest from young hopefuls. Sport, of course, should be approached from two separate directions – competitive and purely for personal fitness ... Sport isn't all about the high achievers and for every gold medallist, there are thousands, probably millions of people who are involved at different levels of participation, observation and actively supporting roles. The latter can often be viewed from the sports widow's perspective and it's often the back-room girls who wash the strips, organise the refreshments, toil in the galley, and nurse broken limbs. Sometimes they are even allowed to socialise at the grand seasonal events ...

How To Arrange a 'Car Boot' Picnic

Anyone who has ever been to a game or agricultural fair, point-to-point meeting, or any other form of rural sporting event, will know the importance of providing a 'good boot'. This is an informal picnic served from the boot of the car – although serving is the only informal thing about it, because there is usually a tremendous amount of preparation involved in the variety and amount of food provided.

What you'll need:

1 dozen mugs
6 whiskey tumblers
6 each knives and teaspoons
1 dozen tea towels
Large picnic basket or hamper
A selection of different sized plastic storage containers
Hot water jugs or a camping kettle
Plenty of napkins

- The experienced rural hostess knows to take plenty of food in order to feed the many 'strays' that turn up uninvited, and there's never a risk of throwing anything away.
- A typical countryman's boot would be expected to offer soup (homemade or good quality tinned – not the soup-in-a-mug variety); hot sausages; sausage rolls; hard boiled eggs; cold chicken; game, egg and bacon, or veal and ham pie; a large selection of sandwiches/rolls with substantial fillings of roast meat or ham; plain rolls and butter, cheese, and large slabs of fruit cake.
- Pack the food, especially cake, sandwiches and rolls, in large plastic storage containers to prevent it from getting squashed. Keep the soup and sausages hot in airtight thermos food jugs. Offer food straight from the container to be eaten with the fingers – plates are not necessary.
- Coffee should be made at the boot as required rather than taken ready prepared – a camping kettle keeps the water boiling – and should be available all day to keep out the cold, often being liberally laced with whisk(e)y. Hot whiskey (see How To Make a Traditional Irish Hot Whiskey – Food & Drink category) and sloe gin is another favourite tipple against the bitter cold.

- Wine is best left to warmer pursuits as chilled Chardonnay can paralyse the bladder, while vintage red brought to impress the guests, can taste like paint-stripper when served in an icy wind in the middle of an open field.
- Don't be too keen to pack up and close the boot until your neighbours do, even if you're frozen to the bone. A lot of socialising goes on after the event has finished while allowing for traffic to clear.

Conclusion

If you're new to this sort of thing, accept any invitations to see how other people run their boot but don't be a 'guest' too often before reciprocating or you'll be looked upon as a free-loader. At these events people do the rounds, so expect to cater for more folk than you actually know. Keep some of the picnic back for a second serving and avoid the embarrassment of running out of food. A well-run boot is part of the social routine at most rural winter sporting events, and can even be found at more urban gatherings such as Twickenham and Goodwood.

Tips:

- Take plenty of tea towels for packing and drying up.
- Don't forget mustard, milk, sugar, pepper and salt.
- People eat with their fingers, so plenty of napkins should be available. Paper is okay, linen is better.
- Don't be snobbish. Offer food and drink to the help, not just the participants.

Warnings:

- If you really want to blend in, don't use a new picnic set with quilted inside and neatly stacking plates and cutlery. Invest in a large battered wicker basket or hamper, and wrap everything in clean, linen tea towels!

- A heavy wax coat and hat with Dubarry boots are the dress code of the day. Few people look elegant on the rural sporting field and warmth is the first priority.

Not really a sports How-To on the surface but there are lots of sporting occasions where the car boot picnic can come in useful – usually because the on-site catering is so appalling. If you watch carefully, you'll find similar arrangements at events such as Silverstone, Ascot and Twickenham where the picnic served from the back of the car is viewed as part of the day's enjoyment (see **Entertainment**). Another area on the periphery of sporting activities is how to take care of sports equipment and how to store it (see **Home**). I can clearly recall my mother washing my father's judo suit and him appearing in the dojo with a beautifully stencilled pink flower pattern across the seat of the trousers where they had come into contact with a damp towel during washing!

Have you any sports How-To's … or how not to's that could be of interest to sports enthusiasts and their families? Or how to encourage children to participate?

Marketplace

Needless to say every sport has its own magazines and newsletters, not to mention its own websites and Facebooks, so plenty of opportunities for How-To material that doesn't infringe on the actual instruction or participation. The disability magazines are also a target market, and in the case of children with disabilities, ·parenting magazines might be interested in a 'how to take up ….' piece if the approach was appropriate. Of course, if you are a keen sports enthusiast then there's nothing to prevent you from offering How-To advice at whatever level you personally participate. There is also a marketplace for the publication of full-length books on sporting activities – with a twist –

such as Jim Dyet's *Straight Down The Middle: Meditation For Golfers.*

Fitness

There are many ways of keeping fit from 'how to choose a personal trainer' to a relaxing, afternoon walk with the dog. Of all the natural stress beaters, regular exercise is one of the best. It helps relieve tension, makes us sleep better, and aids concentration. Moderate exercise also has a beneficial effect on the heart and circulation, and helps ward off illness. In other words, fitness is something we do to keep our minds and bodies ticking over ...

How To Start Running for Fitness and Stress Relief

Providing we introduce ourselves slowly to a new fitness regime, running can help us to get fit, lose weight and help to relieve stress – and we can even do it to music! If you are new to running BUPA has a team of experts to help you get the most from your runs – so go to their website for a free interactive running health check and training programme.

- People often start running to lose weight but they quickly realise that the exercise makes them feel good – less stressed and much happier.
- This is because running pushes blood around working muscles, which can alter stress levels and an emotional state very quickly. And this is why people often feel clearheaded with a more positive perspective on problems after a run.
- Joining a local running club is useful for beginners because it adds to your circle of friends, while instructing you in the correct techniques and how to avoid injury. The most common injuries being to ankles and knees – and usually caused by doing too much, too soon.

- Begin by making the run enjoyable by taking a scenic route while listening to music, which takes your mind off the discomfort in the early stages of running.
- Start your programme by running two or three days in a week for 15-20 minutes walking and running – but not two days in a row to give the muscles a chance to rest after the unexpected exercise. Begin by walking for four minutes, jogging for one, walking for another four and jogging for one.
- To build up to jogging, gradually lessen the time spent walking by one minute and increase the time spent running by one minute each week. Don't push yourself at this stage or it could lead to injury. Run at a sensible pace to begin with, and you will still get all the benefits without the exhaustion.
- A spokesman for BUPA said that the result of feeling calmer doesn't just last for the time of the run but can affect your whole week - particularly if you run regularly - helping you feel more in control and emotionally stronger.
- Some runners take the family dog; others invest in a special running buggy and take the baby. Some find running alone relaxing - while others prefer running in company.
- Apart from the short-term benefits, it is also thought that running provides a sense of achievement and self-confidence.

Conclusion

Recent medical research has revealed that PET scans taken on the brains of people immediately after a run, show endorphins produced during running were stimulating areas of the brain associated with emotion and the feel-good factor. Investing in a specialist pair of trainers can help prevent injury and never ignore pain that is more than aching muscles, consulting your doctor immediately can mean less time spent recovering.

The Health Education Authority maintains that vigorous exercise is not the only way to keep fit and healthy. Research shows that just 30 minutes of physical activity each day – such as walking, or simply climbing the stairs, will keep you fit. Brisk walking and cycling are excellent ways to improve our fitness levels. Many sports and hobbies, such as swimming, dancing, and rambling, have physical benefits as well as being relaxing and stress reducing.

Have you any personal How-To hints on how to make exercise part of our social lives – such as a weekly swim with a friend, or a daily walk with the dog.

Marketplace

With the 2012 Olympics out of the way, there will no doubt be an up-surge of interest in how to keep fit, so lots of opportunities to keep the subject in the news by offering a multitude of ways to improve adult fitness levels and encourage children to participate in competitive sports for enjoyment. Spend an afternoon in the public library with *Willing's Press Guide* and see how many publications you can find that might offer an outlet for your valuable How-To advice ... sports, children and parenting, MB&S, mainstream women's magazines, health and beauty, disability ... and Letters to the Editor, not to mention the full-length opportunities such as Stefan Rippel's *Healing Your Spine*.

Build Your Portfolio

At this stage of building your personal portfolio, we are beginning to push the boundaries in encouraging you to go out and tout for work from local businesses, even if it's only producing their personal promotional leaflets. In *Ghost Writing: How to Write for Others* (Aber Publishing), Lynne Hackles shows how to go about it, and offers some valuable advice on touting for work.

Sport: Exercise 27

Make a list of all the sports clubs in your area and ask if they require promotional leaflets telling beginners (both adults and children) how to take up a new sporting interest. Of course, if you are a sporting participant, then your How-To's can reflect the level you *personally* have attained without compromising professional teaching or coaching. Lynne Hackles, herself a keen cycling enthusiast regularly uses her sport to sell material as she demonstrates in *Writing From Life* (How-To Books).

Fitness: Exercise 28

Fitness, on the other hand, can be something you do unconsciously, which other people may not regard as 'keeping fit'. Running up and down the stairs; a daily cycle ride; a brisk walk (with or without a dog); gardening and vigorous housework can all increase your fitness – how many 'how to keep fit' ideas can you contribute? For example, when we had greyhounds in training we had to walk approx four miles a day, but now they've retired, everyone's quite happy to settle for two miles a day.

Chapter Eighteen

Travel

Everyone has a traveller's horror tale to tell and often it can be turned into a How-To article to prevent others from falling into similar traps. The travel theme is multi-dimensional if we think in terms of holiday insurance, health problems, driving abroad, self-catering hints, travelling with pets, pet passports (see **Pets**), travel for the disabled, elderly people, or those with children. Travel doesn't necessarily mean going abroad, since the trend for home-grown holidays is on the increase, simple How-To tips on economical family get-aways, or away-days, will often have more editor-appeal than a fully-fledged travel article. And those handy How-To hints will always find room in holiday supplements.

How To Avoid Airport Holiday Stress

The worst part of holiday travel is the time we are forced to spend at the airport prior to jetting off to the sun. With a little bit of forward planning, however, there are ways of minimising stress and avoiding the crowds, even if there is a delay in our departure.

- One suggestion is to investigate the possibilities of flying from local airports rather than the major ones, as these tend to offer more convenient and cheaper parking facilities, shorter check-in times and fewer queues. As the airports are smaller, it isn't usually necessary to trek for miles from security check-in to your departure gate; and luggage is off-loaded more quickly on the return journey. If you live in a city near a major airport, check out the feasibility of using another airport - ie. City airport or

Southampton (80 minutes by train from Waterloo) instead of Luton, Stanstead, Gatwick or Heathrow.

- *The Daily Telegraph's* travel correspondent pointed out that if you are booked on a long-haul flight and live in the sticks, you'll probably have to change planes anyway, so instead of flying via Gatwick or Heathrow, consider booking with KLM. This airline has a good network from small British airports to Schiphol – one of Europe's most efficient and best-run airports.

- Remember that airports are generally less congested between 11 am and 4 pm on weekdays, and if you book to fly at these times you may find the fares are more economical too.

- If leaving your car at the airport, check out the region's airports and travel agencies' websites for the special offers within a week or so of your departure. There are all sorts of offers available from reduced rates, valet parking and collection/delivery services, which can dispense with the need to wait for transfer buses, or lug your heavy suitcases about between connections.

- Since most airlines suggest you check-in online and print out your own boarding passes for both the outgoing and return journey, queuing to check in has become a thing of the past. If you need to check in your luggage, make sure you arrive in plenty of time but even this can be eliminated if you travel with hand luggage only.

- Try to avoid the hold-ups at security check-in by paying the fee – although even this is free if you book valet parking through the airport website at Manchester Airport. Check with the relevant airport for details.

- Make sure cabin luggage complies with the size restrictions, which can vary from airline to airline, and the latest security regulations over the number of bags you are allowed. Handbags often count as one piece of luggage and may need to be packed inside the cabin bag. Failure to do so may result in you dumping some of your belongings at the airport before they let you fly.

- Pack so that wet-wipes, make up and toiletries are easily accessible in case of flight delays, so that you can freshen up. Keep a clean top/shirt at the top of the bag in case of spillages, accidents, etc.
- Book access to an executive lounge in advance at a price around £20 per person, so that you can wait in comfort with free soft drinks, toilet facilities, no crowds and no children.
- Alternatively, allow time for a treat when you get through security, i.e. a Gaelic coffee at Shannon, or champagne and smoked salmon at Stanstead – it's the perfect way to start the holiday.

Conclusion

With so many restrictions governing air travel these days, it pays to plan well in advance and minimise the risk of spoiling your holiday before it gets started. Also make sure that you are fully covered by your insurance policy for flight delays and cancellations.

There are so many different dimensions to travel writing and one of these is the constantly changing regulations affecting motoring (see **Motoring**) abroad. A large number of travellers are still unaware of recent changes to France's motoring laws that could involve hefty fines if foreign drivers do not comply. For example, all drivers must carry in their vehicle at all times two officially approved breathalysers ('NF' – *norme française*), which can be purchased from ferry and tunnel terminals. Car hire companies are obliged to provide all necessary equipment but those taking the family car are responsible for ensuring their vehicle complies.A recent survey carried out by Halfords also revealed that one in 10 drivers were not displaying a GB sticker, and one in five did not have headlight converters fitted. French law also requires a vehicle to be equipped with a warning triangle and a luminous safety vest – and that the vest must be inside the car, not in the boot. Drivers are also banned from carrying any device – including satnavs – capable of detecting speed cameras, even if the device is not is use.

Everyone who has ever travelled abroad will have at least one How-To hint to pass on to other travellers going to the same destination. The more we travel the greater out supply of travel tips. Did you know, for example that in Dubai the presence of certain over-the-counter medication in the bloodstream can count as 'possession' and lead to imprisonment?

Marketplace

Travel supplements usually provide up to date information on travel regulation changes, with plenty of advice for making trips abroad less stressful – and all written by seasoned professional travel writers. There are, however, numerous opportunities for travel pieces in local newspapers, women's and parenting magazines, especially in the lead up to the holiday season. Holiday How-To's make good Letters to the Editor, and if you're an experienced back-packer, then 'how to backpack' in China, Australia, Tibet, etc., might be just what a publisher is looking for in a full-length book.

Build Your Portfolio

This is another area where keep it simple is the order of the day but packing advice never goes amiss, especially with all the restrictions on hand luggage. How to purchase the right sized travel bag might save unsuspecting travellers being stopped at check-in because their luggage is only marginally bigger than the maximum allowed. We heard a complaint from a neighbour whose daughter had been forced to throw away some of her clothes before being allowed to board the aircraft because she exceeded the baggage allowance. How to pass through airport check-in with the minimum amount of fuss, might also help those who think that a coat, laptop or handbag doesn't count as 'carry-on baggage'.

Travel: Exercise 29

How to choose the right co-ordinating clothing to fit into a carry-on bag for both men and women could prove helpful. Many of the items would change depending on the age group, destination and length of holiday – so lots of permutations here (see **Fashion** and **Style**). Travel hints to make life less stressful would find space in any holiday supplements, especially if you're writing about travelling with children or the dog? How many How-To ideas can you come up with for this category?

Chapter Nineteen

Weddings & Relationships

When we think about writing about weddings we automatically think about those glossy monthly magazines crammed with expensive meringue-type outfits and chaps in morning dress. Relationships, on the other hand, conjure up the weekly colour magazines brimming over with 'how I discovered my husband was my brother' type of stories, and airing dirty linen ... not surprisingly, my adapted How-To piece from *The Good Divorce Guide* wasn't the usual gowns and tiaras approach.

Weddings

This really *is* thinking outside the box but with more and more people marrying later in life, with careers and personal finances already firmly established, it does make sense to consider a 'pre-nup' ... In fact, some financial advisors are going so far as to claim that if the law is to insist that all assets are split down the middle in the event of divorce, then you might as well run your own personal investments that way from day one of the marriage (see **Personal Finances**). Weddings aren't all doom and gloom so perhaps *you* can come up with ideas that are more in tune with the image of confetti and orange blossom.

How To Consider Making a Prenuptial/Cohabitation Agreement

Often in the news where celebrity couples are concerned, prenuptial and cohabitation agreements are not as legally cut and dried as they may seem. Unlike prenuptial agreements for married couples, cohabitation agreements are recognised by the courts in England and Wales as being legally binding. It is not, however, currently established that prenuptial agreements for married couples are binding in the courts, according to a leading family lawyer. Here are a few points to ponder:

- It is not unreasonable for someone to wish to protect their own personal assets that were accrued before the relationship began, especially in the case of a highly successful and lucrative career, inherited property or family business.
- Faced with the fact that more than one in three marriages finish in the divorce courts, it is becoming increasingly obvious that financial agreements of this nature are necessary.
- Cohabitation agreements are a growing trend among those in the 30-44 age group, largely because these are the people who are more likely to have established a sound financial lifestyle prior to the start of a relationship.
- Although critics (usually female) claim that prenups are the kiss of death to a marriage, those who contemplate this for the second time should seriously consider their position before tying the knot. With the statistics for second marriages being no better than the life expectancy of the first, it is in everyone's best interests to apply a bit of common sense, says *The Good Divorce Guide*.
- Where it is necessary to protect assets gained from a first marriage and to ensure that any children do not loose out in the event of a second marriage breaking up, a prenup is an ideal solution.
- Where a wealthy person remarries someone with considerably fewer financial resources, and wants to protect their assets for any children of a first marriage, some formal agreement would solve any long-term problems.
- Providing there has been a full disclosure of assets before any prenup or cohabitation agreement is signed, and both parties have separate legal representation, courts are less

likely to over turn the arrangement, especially where it safeguards the interests of children.

- Before making any arrangements, draw up a full list of all personal assets accrued prior to the start of the relationship – this should also include any family heirlooms, jewellery, investments, collections, paintings, antiques, etc., that have a monetary value.
- Each of you should consult a solicitor experienced in Family Law as legal proceedings can often be complex and uncertain, so you will need a solicitor to draw up and deal with the paperwork. Your own solicitor will make sure you are not signing away anything you may regret at a later date.

Conclusion

According to the Office for National Statistics, the proportion of unmarried men and women living together has doubled during the past 25 years to about one in eight of the adult population. Providing that you are both in agreement that any prenup or cohabitation agreement is fair and above board, then go ahead and discuss it more fully with your respective solicitors.

Warning

Despite the urban myth that living together for two years automatically qualifies for the same rights as a married couple, a live-in partner does not have an automatic right to inherit their partner's assets.

Continuing on the down-side (which is always much more fun!) there's always the inevitable row about the guest list, wedding presents and seating arrangements. We have a current situation developing that involves the bride making all the arrangements for a plush wedding in Tuscany, while the groom's family is (1) refusing to travel; (2) being unable to travel due to ill-health; or (3) unable to afford the trip. Another friend refused to marry unless the ceremony was held at the old Caxton Hall (now sadly closed), her determined spouse enlisted the help of friends and managed to get around the domiciliary regulations and presented her with a *fait accompli*!

On the plus-side, there are hundreds of hints on how to arrange a value-for-money wedding in these strapped for cash days, to ensure that the couple can still celebrate a special day (see **Family** and **Friends**). How to store a wedding dress ... how to choose the right flowers ... how to preserve a bouquet ... how to economise on wedding cars ... how to get the best value honeymoon ... how to select the right venue ... and how to dress for the big occasion (see **Fashion** and **Style**).

Even the simplest of How-To hints that helps save money without compromising on the 'glamour' is sure to find a sympathetic editor. And don't forget those fabulous 'mother of the bride' outfits that can be found on eBay for a fraction of the original price.

Marketplace

The freelance writer can also join the growing service of writing speeches for the groom, best man or bride's father – or submit a how to (or how not to!) write a speech for a local newspaper's wedding 'advertorial'. Weddings still have a large following if the success of television's *My Big Fat Gypsy Wedding* and *Don't Tell The Bride* is to be believed. Make a study of the bridal magazines and online How-To sites for any potential wedding How-To's and see what you can come up with. And 'how to arrange a wedding ...' must still be one of the popular full-length books in the How-To genre.

Relationships

Relationships cover every permutation of human involvement from that nice old-fashioned term 'courting' couples, to adoptive and step-parents, sibling rivalry, extended families, friendship and neighbours (see **Friends** and **Family**). And the larger our family and circle of friends the more How-To's they will provide – another family 'situation' currently bubbling away is the jockeying for favour with an elderly Uncle with 'loadsa money' to see who can obtain the greater share. Nevertheless, this article was adapted from a short extract in *WLTM: The Dating Game* and offered an insight into what can kill a romance stone dead … the book also included details of 'How To Turn A Woman Off' …

How To Turn a Man Off

There are hundreds of articles advising on how to attract a man, or how to turn him on, but very few detailing what exactly turns him off! During the research for *WLTM: The Dating Game*, the authors discovered that there were some surprising reasons why men didn't come back for a second date. These were the top ten turn-offs…

- Low cut or very revealing clothes, excessive tattooing and body-piercing, and cheap perfume. Simply put, for a large number of males, appearance really does count.
- Women who give the impression that their wide circle of friends, dog/cat/horse, career, and a whole host of other interests come first. In other words, he'll just have to take her as he finds her, or push off. No area of compromise.
- Women who show more interest in a man's life-style with a view to improving their own personal circumstances, rather than discussing mutual interests.
- Poor table manners and flirting with the waiter.
- Women who are aggressive and confrontational without any just cause.
- A lack of humour and raucous laughter seem to rate about equal.
- Talking about ex-lovers, partners or husbands.

- Coarse language and/or conversation peppered with provocative words and statements. If it gives the wrong impression the women only have themselves to blame if the chap tries his hand on the first day!
- An obsession about pets is another area that men find off-putting. Dogs and cats that occupy bedrooms, chairs and sofas won't be approved of by the majority of males. Mentioning that you enjoying dog walking is fine but a whole evening's conversation devoted to a furry friend is definitely out!
- The prospect of assuming responsibility for someone else's children ... although single mums with toddlers seem to fare better than divorcees with teenagers still at home. Unless a man states openly that he likes children, don't assume that he'll be up for playing Happy Families and automatically think your kids are great.

Conclusion

There we have it ... and it's quite a list to think about. This appeared to be a general consensus of opinion from men from all different walks of life but on closer examination, there's very little that women could really take exception to. The authors also discovered that mature men refuse to play mind games and are likely to be more honest about themselves than women of a similar age. Accept the fact that if he's turned off, you're not going to turn him on again.

Relationships in this instance, is mostly about couples – husband and wife, sisters, brother and sister, parents and siblings - and the hundreds of ways they can find between them to make things work – or go wrong. In other words, there is nothing simple in this category that would fit into a mini How-To! And the same rules apply to any other relationships that exist within a family or extended family grouping. We tend to be looking at the 'how to cope with ...' scenarios that plague every permutation of inter-personal relationships. Perhaps a 'how to curry favour with wealthy elderly relatives' might fit in here ... or 'how to cut the rest of the family out of your will' depending on the circum-stances!

What How-To hints can you share to keep life running smoothly? Most family occasions have a spanner thrown in the works at some stage, so what How-To advice can you offer to minimise the damage?

Marketplace

Relationships are the most complex issue on the planet, and most magazines and newspapers build their circulations on the erring and indiscretions of one side or the other. Generally speaking we need to look at the health care, parenting, psychology, lifestyle, Self-Help and religious magazines for market outlets and tailor our How-To advice accordingly. I doubt if there's a family on the planet that hasn't had its fair share of feuding, fall-outs and favouritism, so what sort of How-To can you offer?

Examples of full length titles include Diana and Michael Richardson's *Tantric Love: Feeling vs Emotion*, Chrissie Blaze's *Baby Star Signs*, Caroline Brazier's *Guilt* or Justine Mol's *Growing Up In Trust*.

Build Your Portfolio

There are very few people in this world who have not had some form of relationship with another person, however fleeting, and there are always lessons to be learned for getting things right – or why things go wrong. Most How-To advice seems to focus on patching up quarrels or heading trouble off at the pass ... and if you haven't got any pertinent advice to give, what about the experiences of **Family** and **Friends**. Do remember that you are not breaking any confidences, since How-To advice is not about naming names, the hints and tips are completely anonymous, and there is no need to admit that your cousin Gloria is about to have a sex change – you merely state details of the contacts to be made and the first steps that need to be taken to discover more about the procedure!

Weddings: Exercise 30
Most of us have attended unusual weddings and with the growing choice of venue available to about-to-be marrieds, there's a lot of 'how to arrange a different kind of wedding' opportunities. Or 'how to adapt an old outfit to suit a glam wedding', and 'how to find an unusual but inexpensive wedding gift', if you're thinking from a guest's point of view.

Relationships: Exercise 31
What are the warning signs in your family that a row is brewing? How do you avert the disaster … and help patch things up afterwards? Then there are the eternal how to cope with teenage problems from an untidy room to taking drugs.

Chapter Twenty

Work & Careers

There was a nice story recently on our local radio, where a chap who'd been made redundant from his job as an advertising manager, consulted a specialist to advise on the possibilities of a career change. He wasn't hopeful since advertising was the only job he'd known, and suspected that age had caught up with him in what is essentially a young man's work place. The recruitment specialist told him to go away and ask 12 people what they thought his most positive skills were … the chap was more than surprised at the reactions from friends and former colleagues who considered that he had a wide range of personal skills on which to draw. "Not one of them," he added, "thought I'd make a good advertising manager!"

Work

The same recruitment specialist also made the point that we should not be thinking in terms of looking for a job (employment) but rather be looking for work (freelance). This idea was considered by a friend who was a keen gardener, and had plenty of growing space to provide the bulk of her own vegetables. This How-To was accepted for publication on an online website:

How To Market Home Delivery Vegetable Boxes

The idea of selling boxes of 'delivered to the door' fresh vegetables has been around for a long time but if you have access to lots of home-grown produce, it could be an idea for a small business. Look at what you grow yourself and then look at what the growers on local allotments and market gardens are producing: could this be a family business, or a co-operative. Vegetable box schemes seem to be just as successful in towns, village and rural areas where signing up for a weekly delivery of seasonal produce is something that is looked forward to. Consider the following:

What you'll need:

Plentiful and reliable suppliers
Attractive boxes
Literature for handouts
Tips sheets and recipes
A computer
Reliable transport

- Can you produce/access enough seasonal produce to guarantee a delivery every week of the year? And make it look appetising? A winter box comprising solely of lumpy root vegetables won't tickle anyone's taste buds. What can you offer at this time of the year to keep your customers interested? Never be temped to supplement your stock with bought-in produce from wholesalers - customers will be able to tell the difference and you'll quickly loose their custom.
- It's the fresh, straight from the garden taste that makes the boxes so appealing. Can you include several different types of lettuce, and different sized tomatoes to add interest? Two large beefsteak tomatoes and a bunch of cherry tomatoes on the vine, for example.
- If including anything unfamiliar, such as kohlrabi, be prepared to include a Tip Sheet with information about the vegetable and a couple of suggestions for cooking, otherwise the produce will be wasted. Don't be afraid to offer something new or different, but make sure your customers know what to do with it.
- The advantage of the vegetable box scheme it that the contents have only been harvested one day before delivery,

unlike supermarkets which may keep produce in cold storage for days, weeks or months.

- It's better to convincing a customer to sign up for the scheme in the late spring and summer when there is a much wider selection of fruit, salad and vegetables on offer. Possibly do all your planning during the winter, ready to launch the business in the spring.

- Think about your 'catchment area' and remember that you can't be delivering, gardening and marketing. What other human resources are at your disposal?

- Use standard sized cardboard boxes each week, and use bunches of herbs and vegetable leaves to make it attractive. Offer to remove the previous week's box when you deliver the new one but don't be tempted to recycle dirty or badly stained boxes.

- Prices generally begin around the £8-£9 and until you establish a small customer list don't be tempted to over-reach your capacity for growing or fresh supply. Once you're established, you can offer a deluxe box if your customers want something a little grander – and are willing to pay the extra money for it.

- When travelling around to introduce your service, make sure you take a few vegetable boxes made up to give people an idea of what they can expect. When the round is established, always carry a couple of extra boxes for potential customers who may want to buy there and then.

- Don't be tempted to cover a wide area to start with – start small and gradually build up as your supply chains become more established. Start with a central location and work outwards, rather than picking areas at random that can involved a lot of driving and petrol consumption.

Conclusion

Check out any potential competition on the Internet and check other websites to see what they are offering their customers. There is a nationwide vegetable box scheme operated by Riverford Organic - go onto their sites and see how they do things. Consider adding free-range eggs to the selection if you have access to local farm fresh eggs and including locally homemade jams and preserves to offer during the winter months. Include a weekly A5 recipe sheet with details of future selections.

Starting your own business is always daunting (see **Business**), especially with the banks being less than keen to give loans to small operatives. Nevertheless, we should also be looking at different forms of government allowances schemes and/or tax breaks that can give a modicum of financial assistance for the first couple of years. Here we can also demonstrate how to turn hobbies (see **Pastimes**) into more lucrative ventures, which is what often happens with freelance writers (see **Art**).

Is there any advice you can give – or garner – that can provide sound How-To advice for anyone thinking of starting up their own freelance business?

Marketplace

A How-To outlet for small business magazines and websites – could also be of interest to country or regional publications if there is a local connection. Work is all about selling yourself as a freelance service provider and finding a niche in the community for what you have to offer, with the minimum amount of financial outlay. Plenty of opportunity here for full-length How-To books on specific areas, such as Charlotte Edwards' *Starting a Spiritual Business* - aimed at those with a strong interest in New Age spirituality, or New Age qualifications, and Lawrence Ellyard's *Secrets of Spiritual Marketing* – a guide for natural thera-pists in how to create a successful and profitable business. These two guides illustrate that there *is* a market for full-length books on starting small, home-generated businesses (see **Business**).

Careers

The concept of a job for life is a thing of the past and we have to put a great deal of thought into what we want to get out of life. It's also a subject that's wide open for How-To suggestions on juggling family commitments and a full-time career. In most cases, choosing a career is tempered with ambition – to do something we've always wanted to do (see **Art**); or have a secure financial future. Although the two seldom go together as this particular example shows:

How To Get a Riding Job in a Racing Yard

We've all held our breath as we've watched Keiran Fallon or A P McCoy ride their mounts passed the winning post at Cheltenham or Epsom, and thought 'I'd love to ride racehorses'. If you are a reasonably competent rider, and under 9st 7lbs/60kg in weight this may be easier than you think …

- The first step is accepting that you'll be starting at the bottom of the muck heap – literally – if you apply for a position as a stable lass or lad. Riding out is part of the daily routine – although larger yards do take on casual riders for morning work during the week and on Saturdays. Apply to the racing stables direct.
- Work-riding by comparison, requires a high level of competence in handling more difficult horses, and involves the schooling of horses through the starting boxes, and being used to racing disciplines through riding point to point, former jockeys, etc. Remember that any equestrian sport is dangerous.
- An apprentice jockey also starts on the bottom rung, and will need a combination of riding skills together with an

ability to maintain the right weight for either flat or 'jump' racing, depending on the type of yard.

- The British Racing School at Newmarket originally provided purpose built facilities to promote and encourage young people who had the potential to ride as professional jockeys. Since then, the BRS has developed and flourished to its current position as the centre of excellence for training in the racing industry, providing a whole range of different courses and training, including a 9-week foundation course – see website.

Conclusion

Although the industry isn't particularly well-paid and the hours long, there is a tremendous job satisfaction and camaraderie among the horse racing fraternity that can last a life-time. Study the various different trainers' websites and make a habit of watching Channel 4's *Morning Line* on Saturday mornings.

Giving How-To advice on careers means that we really *do* have to write about what we know, and the above came from my partner who is a former work-rider for some of the best-known trainers in Newmarket. If you are in a position to offer advice from first hand experience then all well and good, but if you've obtained the information from someone you know well, get them to check it out before it goes off for publication. There's nothing in the rulebook that says we can't use other people's input for How-To advice.

How-To advice on careers must be honest – even if it's only telling would-be writers not to give up the day job!

Marketplace

The outlets for these How-To pieces will be more difficult to find because there is no general advice outlet for employment –

although there are plenty of Internet sites that may be worth looking at in specific career areas. Even how to conduct yourself at an interview will vary from company to company (see **Business**); each organisation will have its own yardstick by which an interviewee is measured and what might be good advice for one type of job, could prove counter-productive for another. The target market will be largely dependant on your own background and/or experience. For instance, 'How To Market Home Delivery Vegetable Boxes' might suit any country, regional or gardening publication, whereas 'How To Get a Riding Job in a Racing Yard' would need to be aimed at *specific* equine magazines. Women's and parenting magazines could be interested in how to cope with kids and a career, and for the writer with a solid grounding in these areas, a full-length How-To book might be possible – such as Erin Flynn Jay's *The Mommy Track: Juggling Career and Kids in Uncertain Times*.

Build Your Portfolio

As the last in the book, you would expect these exercises to be a bit more challenging. How-To articles can involve the input of experts in their field to add more muscle to your writing; boost your own freelance opportunities and attract higher fees. But even keeping it simple, we've all worked at *something* during the course of our lives and this must provoke some thoughts on how to exist/survive in the workplace – wherever it was. And in these days of financial hardship, our readers need all the help they can get.

Work: Exercise 32

As we discussed at the beginning of this category, there's a lot of difference between obtaining work and applying for a career. Look at the 'workers' among your family, friends and acquaintances and see what you come up with in terms of a competent How-To piece. Look at how they manage their family affairs and still find time for leisure activities – is there a How-To there? Do other friends supplement their pensions with a little bit of freelance work? What do they do? How do they find work? Are they currently working at something they wouldn't have dreamed of doing some years ago? How did they make the transition?

Careers: Exercise 33

Part of my early career was in advertising and public relations for a multi-national cosmetic company, where I helped produce the monthly 'house journal' that was given to all employees at the plant. My current 'career' is as an author, editor for a creative writing magazine and commissioning editor for a publishing company. My partner has over 40 years experience in racing yards and can be relied upon to provide sound, concise advice as used in the text. This means I can offer How-To advice on just about any aspect of creative writing and publishing ... and most aspects of caring for and riding racehorses ... not to mention the greyhounds. What career experiences can you draw upon? Look at the chapter breakdown example given in the first chapter of *How To Write For The How-To Market* and see if you can produce something similar.

Conclusion: It's a Good Idea, but ...

By the end of this book, you should already have a personal portfolio of over 30 How-To pieces at various stages of construction and publication: articles, fillers, blog and website contributions, online How-To's, letters, and even a possible outline for a book proposal. The secret as we can see, is the ability to think **outside the box** when it comes to selling our ideas to an editor or publisher, and producing something original and/or offbeat. And having discovered the successful formula for writing and presenting How-To material we might find that we have latched onto a long-term niche for marketing our work to run in tandem with our other writing interests.

Believe it or not, this type of writing exercise is also the perfect antidote for what some people would refer to as 'writer's block'. It gives the brain something else to think about while it doesn't want to think about novel writing – and in developing this technique of thinking outside the box, we may find that we unconsciously apply the process of lateral thinking to our fiction writing, too. It's a sort of alternative 'displacement activity' that we can turn to when the next part of that novel just won't come together – after all, there's only so many times we can walk the dogs each day and it beats cleaning the drains!

To be really successful at writing for the How-To market, we need to develop this ability for lateral thinking and, hopefully, the exercises in this book will have encouraged you to think along these lines because it also applies to *all* other areas of creative writing ... including fiction and poetry. Another useful exercise is the method for encouraging lateral thinking taken from business management training of the 1970s, but equally as useful today for the writer who wants to explore new ideas in word-play. 'Mind-mapping' is an idea-generating technique that breaks down linear thinking – thinking in straight lines – and instead of running ideas in a straightforward top-to-bottom listing, we start by placing the key-word in the centre of the page and circling it.

As word association triggers off other ideas, we write them down and circle them, linking them with a line to the key-word; and then linking other compatible ideas with connecting lines. As the circles move outwards, we can travel a long way from the original key-word – and even overlap with another category for additional ideas and opportunities. The longer we carry on with the exercise, we will find we've thrown in things that would never have occurred to us when using a simple ideas list.

As I've observed in *How To Write For The How-To Market* and *Life-Writes*, it's not enough to write on a subject with mere enthusiasm because all How-To, Self-Help and Self-Improvement topics need to reflect 'life as it is lived' by those who have lived it; and imparted to the reader in a way that will encourage them to follow our ideas and guidelines. We can also see from the exercises, that very often there is a cross-category interest and that our idea for – say – 'Art' or 'Pastime' may also cross-pollinate further ideas for 'Work' and 'Business'.

Another thing to consider is the fact that *everything* has a positive and negative aspect, so if you find that writers' submissions are focussing on the up-side of a subject, turn things on their head and look at it from the down-side. Look at the different examples given in the text and reverse the viewpoint – is there a How-To piece that you could produce by taking the opposite stance – such as *How Not To Write A Novel* by Sandra Newman and Howard Mittelmark (Penguin). Instead of 33 How-To items in your portfolio, a flip of the mind could give you 66! Have a try!

So far, we may not have earned a lot of money for our efforts, but we will have an impressive portfolio to start our 'How-To writing career. Keep copies of everything you have submitted but remember that it cannot go into your portfolio until it has appeared in printed or online published form. Don't be afraid of rejections, as these are all part of the learning curve ... and so is having the courage to submit material for a stranger's scrutiny in the first place.

Bear in mind that even the most experienced of us still receive rejection slips. It doesn't necessarily mean that our material is no good; the editor may have already published something similar, or have commissioned an almost identical idea from another writer. It isn't possible to check on all the back-issues of magazines but we *can* check out the contents of the How-To websites and see what they have previously accepted from our rivals in the How-To stakes. And a trawl through the websites' categories may stimulate other ideas *we* can use elsewhere after all, there's no copyright on ideas.

If, however, you've got to the end of this book and had difficulty in *writing* at least 20 How-To's for publication, then we need to go back to the drawing board. Have you explored the full market potential for every one of the categories listed in the text? Where did you look? On the shelves of your local newsagent? The library? The secret behind selling non-fiction material is all about the amount of effort you are willing to put in to discover new outlets for your work. If you're casting your line over the same tired old publications, hoping for a nibble, it may be a long time before you land your catch.

Market research never appears to be very high on writers' 'things to do' lists but this is exactly what gives us the edge over our rivals. If we compare the number of market outlets listed in the various writers' handbooks, with those in the mega-entry *Willings Press Guide*, we will discover more markets in the English-speaking world than we could write for in a life-time. Only a very small number of publications appear in the handbook listings, while *Willings* covers regional and national newspapers, magazines, periodicals and online publications in three separate volumes for the UK, Europe and the rest of the

World. Copies can be found in central libraries' reference sections and a couple of hours browsing will provide dozens of outlets for your How-To material. **Markets don't come to you, you have to go out and search for them** ... even create them if necessary by approaching local free papers and suggesting you provide them with 'advertorials' when they are planning special features.

If, on the other hand, the problem is disinterest from the editors, it probably means that you are not producing original, thought provoking ideas, or that your approach is not compatible with the publication's house-style. Studying the actual publications and emulating the writing style of previously published material can improve the latter. If the difficulty is related to the former, then it requires a great deal of effort in developing your way of thinking about a subject. This type of writing requires a tremendous leap of the imagination but once you get to grips with automatically thinking outside the box, the easier the ideas will flow – and you'll never think in straight lines again.

**COMPASS
BOOKS**

Compass Books focuses on practical and informative 'how-to' books for writers. Written by experienced authors who also have extensive experience of tutoring at the most popular creative writing workshops, the books offer an insight into the more specialised niches of the publishing game.